CONTENTS

RELAXING IN THE SKIES ABOVE THE ISLAMIC STATE

.

Bored with the movies, and slipping into that half-awake state common for long flights, I switch the entertainment screen to locate myself in the world. Arcing across the globe, I am flying from Australia to Europe, a 24-hour haul. As I stare at the screen, the borders strike me. They are lines, drawn in ink, but so much blood has been spilled over them. The map tells me we are now over Iraq. A country, like so many others in the Middle East, concocted on a map. As the plane on the screen inches forward toward our destination, dots representing cities come into view. Then, there it is—Mosul, a city of nearly two million. The great seat of the Christian church in the Middle East for centuries, now under the Islamic State's control.

I look around the cabin. Glowing screens puncture the dark. People doze, watch movies, eat food, request stewards. Below us in Mosul, people are screaming. Medieval torture, genocide, and slavery descend upon the people like dragons. But in this sealed, sacred, purified space, thousands of feet in the air, we are as free as birds.

I fall into an uneasy sleep.

Waking later, my screen still shines. As my eyes focus, I see that we have left the Middle East and now are making our final swing across Eastern Europe. We are above Ukraine, and I think again of the conflict below. Another dispute tumbles into violence, driven by those lines, borders marking who's in and who's out.

I continue midair philosophizing on our two-level world, where the global elite fly comfortably while children of the dust fight famine and fall asleep to the sound of gunfire. I look at the walls of the plane, a thin metallic membrane, a border to protect us from the chaos below. I wonder to myself, *Is it safe to be flying over these conflict zones?* It must be. Surely the airlines and the governments of the developed world wouldn't let us if not.

A few hours later, freshly landed on the ground and ensconced in the safety of Northern Europe, I catch the cable news. Another Malaysian Airlines jet has gone down—shot down, I'd later learn, over a conflict zone. The plane had been traveling opposite of mine, at roughly the same time, filled with fellow Australians and other nationalities. Torn from the sky. That thin skin, that fragile membrane of security, peeled away. I shake my head. *The world is going mad.*

WHAT IN THE WORLD IS GOING ON?

The globe seems to be moving into a phase of disruption. "Order has unraveled," writes Richard Haass, president of the Council on Foreign Relations. "The balance between order and disorder is shifting toward the latter."[1] For Haass, this is not a trend that will be resolved anytime soon. "Left unattended, the current world turbulence is unlikely to fade away or resolve itself. Bad could become worse all too easily." Are upheaval and chaos the new norm?

Daily we are faced with a barrage of mad, bad, and confusing news. A constant stream of visceral video delivered to our screens. An ISIS operative exploding at a Belgium airport, the victim of a police shooting bleeding to death live on Facebook, the president of Turkey mid-coup asserting his power via Facetime, images of an aid worker picking up the body of a Syrian toddler washed up on a resort beach. *Warning: some viewers may find the following footage disturbing* is becoming the tagline of our moment.

How do we view this pivotal moment in global history through biblical lenses? The church is called to be an embassy of the kingdom, to be salt and light in the world, a vision of a Spirit-filled alternative. Believers are humans, and humans are social creatures profoundly influenced and molded by the culture around us. Fear, worry, and anxiety are socially infectious. Scripture tells us that we are not to be a people of fear, but of love, power, and a sound mind. How can we be light on a hill as darkness seems to fall? What is it to live a life in the Spirit in a moment of anxiety, upheaval, and extremes? We will get to these questions, but let us first consider why it feels as if our world is in chaos and turmoil, starting with a brief look at the media.

The Role of Media

There's a scene in the 2015 film *The Big Short* where actress Margot Robbie, soaking in a bubble bath, succinctly explains the 2008 global financial crisis. Faced with the difficulty of communicating its economic complexities, director Adam McKay chose Robbie to deliver what could have been the most boring dialogue. The scene is emblematic of our moment of cultural anxiety. We feel the effects of globalization, yet its full meaning eludes us. It is simply too easy to be distracted. *"Lehman Brothers? Junk bonds? Subprime mortgages? Sorry, I was looking at the beautiful girl in the bath."* The medium drowns the message in the bathwater. The way we *receive* information—primarily through cable news and the Internet, which are instant and blended with entertainment—is changing how we *perceive* information, and thus, how we experience the world.

Our mental environments daily become a confusing blend of horror, distraction, and fun. Our portable devices mean that we are always receiving a torrent of information. Checking Facebook for the details of a party invite, one can see news about a terrifying event half a world away. "For most of history, news was so hard to gather and expensive to deliver, its hold on our inner lives was inevitably kept in check,"[2] reflects philosopher Alain de Botton. Now, however, it is everywhere. The contemporary landscape allows our every glance to constantly find screens, and on those screens, a constant flow of news. "The hum and rush of the news have seeped into our deepest selves,"[3] says de Botton.

Media theorist Douglas Rushkoff describes the way we now interact with media as *present shock*. In present shock, all that matters is what is happening right now. In the past, news worked in cycles. When a late-breaking event occurred too close to print, it'd be in the next day's paper. But in our new streaming reality, news breaks live. The first tweet, the live video, embedded reporters on the scene—the continual present keeps flooding in.

"Blatant shock is the only surefire strategy for gaining viewers in the now," observes Rushkoff, who points out that this media stream creates an emotional response in us. The constant media news cycle

> make[s] good business out of giving voice to our presentist rage. Opinionated, even indignant, newsreaders keep our collective cortisol (stress hormone) levels high enough to maintain a constant fight-or-flight urgency. Viewers too bored or impatient for news reporting and analysis tune in to evening debate shows and watch pundits attack one another. The pugilism creates the illusion of drama, except the conflict has no beginning or end—no true origin in real-world issues of legitimate effort at consensus. It's simply the adaptation of well-trodden and quite obsolete Right-Left debate to the panic of a society in present shock.[4]

In this media culture, *punditry replaces analysis*. Facts float. Feelings replace truth. News becomes a visceral rather than cerebral medium. Events at hyperspeed are debated and rapidly placed in preexisting ideological categories of left and right. The constant rush of present shock, which delivers geysers of information but little understanding, only adds to the chaos.

That said, even if the news media were entirely calm and collected, if it triple-fact-checked every report, if it perfectly followed the laws of healthy discourse in every interview—and if we only took news in every now and then—we still could not escape the fact that the world is in a state of unrest. What follows is only a sampling of the issues in our current global moment.

Terrorism and Cartels

The Iraqi branch of Al-Qaeda has morphed into what is known as the Islamic State, a swift and terrifying terrorist group. The insurgent amoeba captured large swathes of Iraq and Syria, turned its hand to the building of its own Islamic state, declaring it a caliphate, the geographical area under the control of the leader of the world's Muslims. The group's ability to use social media, combined with its brutal and sadistic tactics, has horrified the world. They've launched operations in cities like Paris and Berlin, and they've weaponized mental illness and social isolation to produce lone-wolf attackers, creating an atmosphere of fear and fragility in the West.

Due to the connected, cut-and-paste nature of our world, gangs and cartels have begun adopting terrorist tactics. Through back channels and black markets of the globalized economy, organizations like the Sicilian Mafia and Mexican drug cartels are building empires of crime, networks profiting off narcotics, counterfeit goods, weapons smuggling, and human trafficking.

Refugees, Immigrants, Walls, and Borders

Large populations are on the move, driven out of their homelands by war, oppression, and economic and environmental distress. The movement of refugees has become a political conflict across the world. In almost every continent, concerns over refugees and illegal border crossings have meant more walls being built and proposed.

Economic implications accompany this. With population declining, particularly in developed countries, current models of welfare are vulnerable, because they were created in times of prosperity. Thus, politicians look to immigration to boost population and ensure a viable taxation base. However, in periods of economic stagnation, and amid the decline of manufacturing in the West, increasing friction occurs between local populations and recently arrived migrants.

The policy of multiculturalism, in which migrant populations are encouraged to retain and nurture their cultures, has come under increasing critique. Frictions are felt between migrants with traditional values and local populations committed to Western progressive values (particularly in regard to sexuality, gender, and religious issues). Western leaders such as Germany's Angela Merkel have thus declared the death of multiculturalism, creating mechanisms to conform migrants' values to those of majority culture. This move is another sign of increasing cultural tension in the West, forcing the West to ask the question, *"What is it to be Western?"*

Corruption, Failing Institutions, Leaks, and Elites

In the last decade, a series of scandals involving elites has erupted. Between Wikileaks, Edward Snowden, the Panama Papers, corruption in the Brazilian government, and the hacking of the Democratic National Committee's emails, public trust in governments is increasingly eroding.

The 2008 global financial crisis also eroded trust. Decades of risky behavior and corrupt practices among leading financial institutions finally came to a head, bursting into a crisis that brought whole countries to the brink of economic catastrophe. The effects are still being felt today, especially in the political atmosphere. The sense among the public is that elites, with their hands on the levers of the world economy, are amoral and disconnected from reality. But these rolling institutional failures go beyond just governments and banks. Scandals involving systematic sexual abuse have also reared their heads, from the Catholic Church to certain British celebrities. Even the great global sporting institutions get embroiled in controversy.

Confusing Conflict and Dirty Wars

In the last decade, Syria, Iraq, Libya, and Yemen have descended into quagmires of conflict, contributing to a rise in terrorism around the world (and with that, a massive refugee crisis). The sheer complexity of these conflicts can boggle the mind. Rebels employed by various factions, terrorist ideologies, ethnic and religious backgrounds, mercenaries, political ideologies, and foreign powers all join the battle. Multiple sides exist, shifting allegiances. No clear concept of victory exists.

The conflict in eastern Ukraine brought another word into our lexicon of modern conflict: *dirty war*. When masked troops in unmarked uniforms began appearing in eastern Ukraine, the media dubbed them "the little green men." At first, the Russian government denied that they were Russian troops. Later, Vladimir Putin would concede that Russian *Spetsnaz* (special forces) were indeed engaged in Ukraine. Dirty war and asymmetrical conflict are increasingly used by rising international powers such as Russia, Turkey, and Iran, who wish to wield power beyond their borders but do not have the power to challenge the United States in a conventional war. Dirty wars are conflicts that engage not only conventional military force, but also propaganda, disinformation, cyber warfare, and criminal elements, to gain advantage. The use of such techniques only intensifies the division growing in our world.

Total Culture Wars

The concept of culture wars originated in Germany and other European countries in the mid- to late-nineteenth century when liberalizing nation states attempted to roll back the social and political influence of the Roman Catholic Church. The resistance of the Church was termed the *Kulturkampf* (English, *culture struggle*), a conflict pitched as a struggle between secularizing forces and Christian culture. Now, however, many of the culture wars emerging are framed as struggles between the influence of Islamic culture and secularism. This clash concerns matters like Islamic swimwear or "burkinis," public prayer, the place of halal food in the public square, and the wearing of the veil.

These disputes over the culture of Islamic minorities are not limited to Europe. They also occur in places like Burma, Sri Lanka, and Trinidad and Tobago. Even in the Middle East and Eastern Europe, heated disputes often break out online over the influence of Americanism, Western values, and even Chinese values, creating new fronts of cultural conflict. *The Guardian* newspaper has reported on the growth of a far-right movement in Mongolia, which strangely embraces Hitler, and rejects what it sees as the foreign influence of China.[5] Professors in Ghana have called for the removal of local statues of the Indian peace activist Gandhi, decrying him as a racist, stating that "it is better to stand up for our dignity than to kowtow to the wishes of a burgeoning Eurasian super power."[6] No longer are the culture wars binary engagements conducted by two forces. They are global, multi-front, asymmetrical wars, creating an atmosphere of constant cultural flashpoints.

Political Polarization

The incursion of politics into areas of everyday life has led to the sense that everything is politicized. Due to increased activism, more and more schools, corporations, and even athletic organizations are wading into the political arena, creating a large field of dispute in the public sphere. Increased activism on both the left and right, plus the ability to target and dispute the political content of nearly anything—online especially—has spread the conflict.

The very nature of political debate has also become fractured and feverish. The ability to consume TV programs, blogs, websites, and Twitter accounts already in accord with one's political viewpoints naturally clusters the like-minded. As communal life moves into a more individual form, and community is found online, we can avoid encountering and relating to those who think differently. With the crisis facing print media, one strategy for gaining online traffic has been to have partisan commentators generate debate in comment sections. Thus the media is less inclined to promote a neutral tone, and instead has moved toward firebrand commentary. It also gives extreme activists wider audiences and influence. Online campaigns spread like wildfire—good news for those wishing to change the world positively, bad news when you consider that extremists exploit the Internet to harass, target, shame, and troll. Such tactics are poisonous to political and social discourse, cultivating division and distorting truth.

Disconnection in Our Connected World

In a microsecond we can connect with friends, family, and coworkers across the globe. The paradox, though, is that the tool that offers us incredible social connectivity can also isolate us. Emerging online technologies offer broad social networks yet struggle to offer the deep connections essential to human well-being. Adding to the sense of fragility is the wane in traditional notions of family. Radical individualism continues to dominate, and more and more adults are living alone. Our increasing connectivity to more people, more news, and more opinions, alongside our relational poverty, can make us feel disconnected and estranged from others. In turn, this can lead to anxiety and worry about our own lives and the fate of our world.

* * * * *

This is a challenging number of issues, for sure. What is more, the nature of each issue is quite different. Some are political, social, cultural, religious, and even technological, and others are a combination of several. Add in the fact that these issues span the globe and concern cultures and people we don't understand, and the whole of it can be dizzying. However, if we begin to look deeper, underneath these conflicts and tensions, we see a spider web of borders and boundaries—clashes over place, identity, and meaning. As we will discover, there is a pattern behind this chaos.

To discover this pattern, we need a road map. In Part 1 we consider the biblical pattern of chaos. *Where does chaos come from? What are the basic forces operating? How does what happens in Scripture inform what is happening in the world?* In

Part 2 we consider the historical pattern of chaos. *How can we map what we know from Scripture and the spiritual factors at play in the world to the specific movements occurring all around us? How can we perceive the spiritual dimensions of war, terrorism, the breakdown of the family, technology and isolation, and other issues?* Part 3 concludes the book by exploring how what the New Testament calls life in the Spirit offers an alternative to the chaos of our times. *What does it mean to live in light of Christ's victory over the flesh and elemental forces? How do we live life in the Spirit, embodying the presence of Jesus in our homes, communities, and the world?* My goal is to grasp our cultural moment, to help you understand its landscape. There is a pattern to the chaos, and what is more, there is a door out, into the holy expanse that is life in the Spirit.

PART 1

BIBLICAL PATTERN OF CHAOS

CHAPTER ONE

FROM EDEN
TO THE EAST

At dawn of an August morning, 1978, Prince Michael Bates of the principality of Sealand personally led a daring mission to recapture his nation from invading German and Dutch mercenaries. The operation was successful, and no one lost their life. Following negotiations with German and Dutch government officials, Prince Michael released the invaders he had held as hostages, and he was free to rule his homeland. Yet another example of the habit of humans throughout history to risk our lives to defend, and fight for, our homes, nations, and kingdoms.

Sealand, however, was no ordinary country. And Prince Michael was no ordinary royal. Sealand is what is termed a *micronation*. A former World War II anti-aircraft platform, located several miles off the English coast in the North Sea, the dilapidated concrete and metal platform is slightly smaller than a basketball court. Lying abandoned, it was claimed in the 1960s by entrepreneur and pirate radio operator Roy Bates, who declared it his own kingdom. He even printed his own money and passports and created his own flag. Media footage from the early days of Sealand shows Bates commanding himself with all the self-importance of a monarch, while his wife, Joan, looking regal and full of adoration, leans in to his side. Their self-confidence as rulers contrasting with the ramshackle surrounds of the rotting platform in which they hold court.

Sealand could appear as a joke, or an excuse for a tax dodge, but for a half-century the Bates family has defended Sealand, most notably when rival businessmen hired goons to seize the platform while Roy was away on business. Armed with firearms, and with the aid of their friend, a former James Bond stuntman and helicopter pilot, the Bates family willingly risked their lives to recapture their micronation. Illustrating the way in which humans are seemingly wired to create places, to erect borders around them, and to be willing to defend them with our lives. This impulse of humans to create "places" is vital to understand if we are to grasp our current cultural moment. The Scriptures are a wonderful place to begin to discover why we seek a place called home.

THE FIRST PURE SPACE

Whether we are believers or not, the boundaries and structures of secularism shape and form the way we think about religion. The devout can buy into the myth of the sacred-secular divide, unconsciously relegating faith into the private realm. Thus we struggle to see that the whole of culture operates in the grammar of religion. Yet if we are to be biblical people, we must learn again to view the world through the lens of Scripture. To again turn to Scripture's wisdom, which divides soul and spirit, laying bare the motivations of the human heart. Such motivations, the origins of human possibility, tragedy, and failing are found in the book of Genesis—a book that shows that all human history is colored with a religious hue.

Genesis presents all of creation as a temple, and humans as divinely ordained priests. Whereas we are used to thinking of temples as buildings, God originally established the whole world as a temple. The divine, the sacred, was not confined to brick and mortar.

The early scenes of the Bible show us a God who is gloriously powerful and omnipotent, who can speak universes into being, a cosmic God, above and beyond the parochial gods who guarded small areas of earth and served tribes and nations of humans. He is the God of the world. He is both radically present yet separate from His handiwork. Present in the good creation He inhabits, He walks in the garden in the cool of the day. He's a relational Deity, capable of conversation and communion. Humans are created to be His partners in conversation, to bask and worship in His presence. He tasks them as His functionaries, stewards or priests. Their identity is rooted in their Creator and the vocation He has given them, to flourish as they ensure that creation flourishes.

Adam and Eve's place is with God and in the world, because everything is in its right place. The world operates as God intended it to. Creation praises Him as it performs the roles He has given it. God is not restricted to a temple, confined to a building, because the whole world operates in the tenor of worship; everything points toward Him. Heaven is where

God's will is obeyed, thus there is no delineation between heaven and earth. Reflecting God's good order, a series of borders exists to ensure the flourishing of creation. The border between Creator and creation. Between humans and animals. The border that prevents humans from eating from the Tree of Knowledge of Good and Evil, preventing the priests from futility and disastrously attempting to cross the border between humanity and divinity.

Yet these priests stage a coup. Those who worship wish to become objects of worship themselves. The serpent promises the potential to become like gods. When Adam sinks his teeth into the fruit, a sacred boundary is transgressed. Humans trade eternal life with God for the weakness of mortality.

Humanity is expelled from the garden, separated from easy access to God's presence. A new order is established, one with cherubim as border guards. Peter Leithart writes, "After Adam's expulsion from the garden, holy space became taboo, inaccessible space."[1] Thus humanity finds itself wandering east of Eden, aware at a deep level that it is expelled, yet also aware that Eden exists. The space of true freedom, of true communion with the divine, where humans are truly recognized as His children, able to approach God without fear, to commune with Him freely, to see each other minus the lens of sin, is no longer accessible. Instead, their fate: God's judgment has them exposed, vulnerable to the forces of chaos that they themselves have participated in unleashing.

SCRATCHING OUT EDEN IN THE DUST

Because humans are spiritually homeless, we dream of holy spaces, utopias, motherlands, golden ages, and soulmates. We yearn for reconnection to the divine, re-admittance to the sacred and pure space. "The seed of all of man's questing is to be found in Cain's life in the land of wandering, always searching for a place where his need for security might be satisfied,"[2] observes Jacques Ellul. This wandering, this lostness, is the essence of humanity's essential weakness: *detachment from their true home in God, and with that, the curse of mortality.*

With this detachment—this sense that we have a true home but are not living in it—we see in a myriad of ways that something is awry in the world, that it is tainted, impure, and corrupted. Death, disease, and disorder lurk, bursting out at points. Cain's response to this situation of danger, fear, and dislocation is outlined in Genesis 4:16–17: "Then Cain went out from the LORD's presence and lived in the land of Nod, east of Eden. Cain was intimate with his wife, and she conceived and gave birth to Enoch. Then Cain became the builder of a city, and he named the city Enoch after his son."

Cain, just as all humans will do, fights back against his weakness and mortality with an attempt to carve out meaning and legacy apart from God. First, he and his wife conceive a son. While God had commanded Adam and Eve to procreate and fill the earth, the tone of Cain's act of procreation carries a different tenor. It is the attempt to strike back at mortality by creating a line of descendants, to reach beyond the impending grave with a glorious lineage. As Ellul writes, "It is man's desire to find life, eternity, again. He transmits his life to his children . . . He will satisfy his desire for eternity by producing children."[3]

After his wife gives birth to a son, Cain attempts to create a legacy by creating a city named after his son. God had named Adam—a display of authority over the man. Yet Cain wished to exercise his own name-giving power, attaching it not just to his own son, but to a city. Cain, like his parents, attempts to be like God. Not just in exercising the power of name-giving, but in exercising power over life in the murder of his brother Abel. Erasing the brotherhood of humanity, by erasing his brother from the world. This act of domination, of the taking of life and the making of life, makes possible the establishment of the first city.

Building the city, too, is an act of subtle rebellion against God. It is an attempt to mirror the security and peace of Eden, but without God. It was a projection of human power, an attempt to counter the weakness of mortal human flesh with the solidity of stones and walls. "The city is almost certainly founded on the fear of death and with a view to safety," Leon Kass notes.[4]

Cain reaches for a kind of substitute for eternity by fathering a son and attempting to create a lineage. He initiates a city in his son's name, but without the protection of God. Fear grips him; his lineage, his memory, must be protected, so he creates a city, a location protected by walls and a watchtower—a memorial to himself and his family and protection against chaos in the world.

Like Cain, our selfish rebellion, thrusting us into the fleshly condition of fear and mortality, seeks to find security and stability in the spaces, places, and social structures that we create.

Lost, wandering east of Eden, we, like Cain, scratch out imitations of home in the dust of where we find ourselves. Unable to return to Eden, we create a place for ourselves.

CHAPTER TWO

THE NATIONS RAGE

At 9:36 pm on July 13, 1977, New York City experienced a citywide blackout. Those who were there for the 1965 blackout remembered how civilly everyone responded then. Neighbor helped neighbor, and a community spirit defined the event. This time it was different. The social fabric was fraying. The city was straining from the nation's economic woes. Poverty was rampant, and cost-cutting measures slashed essential community services. When the lights went out, havoc erupted. Looting and arson spread across the city. When even ordinary citizens joined in, the power of mob mentality was revealed. Soon looters were looting other looters. By sunrise thousands had been arrested, over a thousand buildings had been torched, and hundreds of police officers were injured. Total damages ran into the hundreds of millions. Some retail strips didn't recover for over a decade, as store owners boarded up their businesses, unable to face the prospect of selling to the neighbors and friends who had looted their stores.

The darkness threw a blanket over law, order, and social convention. Within minutes the social fabric unraveled. What was formerly strength in numbers became danger in numbers. The darkness, paradoxically, cast a light upon the motivations of the human heart. We see the tensions between our human social systems, created to protect us, and their propensity to tear at us. This is something at play in our world today, something the Scriptures are deeply interested in.

COALITIONS OF THE FLESH

Psalm 2 gives a realistic view of world affairs, pondering the struggle between earthly authorities and the heavenly King. "Why do the nations rebel and the peoples plot in vain? The kings of the earth take their stand, and the rulers conspire together against the LORD and His Anointed One: 'Let us tear off their chains and free ourselves from their restraints'" (Ps. 2:1–3).

Even now, the Hebrew word for the nations, *goyim*, is often uttered with a desultory sting, because the nations were Israel's enemies. They would surround, oppress, and enslave God's people. Whereas Israel would fail its priestly vocation by falling into idol worship, the nations are another matter. Like a wild bull, they buck at the restraints that God has placed upon them for their and the world's safety. (A sobering thought to reflect upon as we stand for our national anthems.)

The nations and their rulers plot rebellion against God's ordered plan. "These are not just kings but 'earth's kings'— kings from all over the world," reflects John Goldingay. "This is not just an ordinary, small-scale rebellion but the whole world asserting itself."[1] Nations are a melding of people, place, and culture. Biblically, they emerge organically from the rebellion of Babel, the great human project to ascend to the heavenly heights of divinity by human effort, to continue the rebellion of Adam and Eve "to become like gods" via great and heroic human endeavors. They are a response to our mortal, weak, and fleshly existence, an effort at having strength and protection in numbers, solace and comfort in community, meaning in language and culture. To insulate the human heart against the cosmic loneliness and insecurity that humanity experiences after the fall.

But at the heart of these coalitions is a contradiction: we attempt to escape the flesh by gathering it together. The structures, communities, and institutions we create in order to protect ourselves from the chaotic ravages of the flesh do not free us from the effects of the flesh. For the flesh is within us. Augustine reminds us:

> Indeed, it may happen that a man refrains from sensual indulgence because of devotion to an idol, or because of the erroneous teaching of some sect; and yet even then, though such a man seems to restrain and suppress his carnal desires, he is convicted, on the authority of the apostle of living by the rule of the flesh; and it is the very fact of his abstention from fleshly indulgence that proves that he is engaged in the "works of the flesh."[2]

In other words, what we create to protect ourselves from the flesh can also end up serving the flesh.

Law and order, our traditions and social conventions, our governance, are created to protect us from being overrun by the flesh. We build militaries and borders to protect us from the evil outside us. We create police forces, legal systems, and punishments to protect us from the evil within. We intuitively grasp that if we are to flourish, love, create, and build, we must be protected from the flesh that always lurks both within and without. Thus our cultures contain the chains of which Psalm 2 speaks—the restraints that we create to protect us from the flesh. They are on one hand God-given, yet they also have the potential, when disconnected from their divine source, to become overrun by the flesh themselves.

Ancient civilizations, nations themselves, seemed to have a fairly perceptive view of the danger of the flesh. The Greeks and Romans feared the decay and corruption that luxury and comfort brought. The Greek historians Herodotus and Xenophon both worried that cultures that enjoyed soft living eventually were overrun by more militant peoples toughened by deprivation. Aristotle attempted to protect Greek civilization by discouraging young men from political service, because wealth and comfort would disconnect them from the common experience and cause them to view life through the prism of pleasant feelings.[3] The Roman writers Cato and Juvenal acted as watchdogs over the moral state of the Empire, fearing that the comfort and indulgence engendered by its success would sap its strength. Tacitus looked favorably upon the "barbarian" Germanic tribes, lauding them for their sexual ethics in comparison to what he called the "modern" sexual culture of promiscuity in Rome.[4] Polybius, one of the great observers of Roman culture, fretted that the decadent sexual and materialistic mores of his Greek culture were corrupting the strength and vitality of the Roman Republic.

Thus the wisdom of the ancient world tended to side with the view that social and political progress would eventually be sabotaged by the frailties of human nature. History was a perpetual cycle, a fight of civilization against flesh, a struggle that would ultimately be undone from within. The ancients worried that their culture, weakened and degraded, would eventually be overrun by the barbarians who always seemed to be amassing at the border, threatening to sack civilization in a kind of deserving failure. A protecting force was needed. The borders could not be breached.

The strategies of Rome for protecting against the flesh were trade, commerce, stability, freedom of religion, liberty, and the flourishing of classical culture and philosophy. Yet, this was enforced with the *gladius*, the sword of the legionaries, designed to smash skulls and disembowel those who resisted the reign of peace. When the North Africans of Carthage dared to take the fight to Rome, crossing the impenetrable Alps to the empire's borders, the armies of Rome fought them all the way back to North Africa. Defeat was not enough; they crushed Carthage. They sold its citizens into slavery, burned their city, and salted their fields so none would yield crops ever again. The Roman military machine wiped Carthage from the face of the earth—an entire culture obliterated by the legions of flesh.

And so, a cycle emerges, a self-defeating vortex. Our nations, our cultures, our places, and indeed our religions—buffers against the flesh—soon turn into barriers distancing us from God, which is an essential component *of* the flesh. These systems take on a life of their own and go rogue, becoming destructive rather than protective forces.

LONGING TO BE HUMAN

"The sin of man consists in that he does not want to be flesh," writes Herman Ridderbos, reminding us that we are defined by our rebellion against God. We hate our mortality, our weakness, so even as we battle against flesh, we wish to transcend it. Our desire to be as gods continues beyond Eden. The human "does not want so to be flesh as it has been given to him to be, as the foundation of a life after the will of God."[5] In God's plan, the limitations of our flesh turn us to Him. Sensing our weakness, we long for strength. Fearing our mortality, we desire to live forever. God is the answer to both these needs—and more—so that, in His wisdom, our flesh creates a longing only He can fulfill.

But when we seek fulfillment elsewhere, we use the flesh to try and fulfill desires of the spirit—we take up attitudes and actions that oppose the reign of God in our lives, further adding to our chaos. Our flesh blinds us. Our minds are driven into a kind of madness, warped by the terror of our fleshly limitations. We begin our rebellion against God, conspiring between each other, but our conference of fleshly rebellion is futile. *Flesh next to divinity is revealed for what it truly is.* For "The One enthroned in heaven laughs; the Lord ridicules them" (Ps. 2:4). We are deservedly mocked, for our great programs to rid the world of flesh too often create more flesh.

The good news, however, is that God is no cynic who delights in human misery and mayhem. Instead, He has a plan. Psalm 2 speaks of a Davidic earthly king whom God chooses and promises, "I will make the nations Your inheritance and the ends of the earth Your possession" (Ps. 2:8). This is no king of the world who rebels against God and sows discord. Instead, this King is God's Son, ruling from God's holy mountain. Facing this King, the fleshly kings of the world are counseled, "Be wise; receive instruction, you judges of the earth. Serve the LORD with reverential awe and rejoice with trembling" (Ps. 2:10–11). The earthly kings, should they rebel against Him, will perish in their rebellion.

That King came, but not as most kings do. Born in poverty to parents on the run, and raised in obscurity ("Can anything good come out of Nazareth?" [John 1:46]), He defied earthly notions of kingship and power, confounding humanity with His humility. The role of kingship is a dramaturgy, using the symbols of power—thrones, palaces, scepters, harems, crowns, ostentatious displays of wealth and might. Jesus' saving act upon the cross, the confirmation of His kingship, the axial point of salvation history, is filled with royal imagery, but all of it is turned on its head.

There is no grand procession to a palace, only a painful march outside the city. No royal fragrances or incense, only the stink and waste of rotting garbage. No resplendent throne inlaid with the plunders of an empire, only a common cross made for anyone. No golden crown of shining jewels, only thorns digging into flesh. No royal wine flowing in celebration, only blood and water spilling from His side. No torches or parades, only a cosmic darkness. No cheers, only the sobs of the women standing at a distance, faithful to the gory end.

The Hebrew prophets had predicted His appearing, and the people of God had prayed, waiting in painful anticipation for the coming of the Messiah. For the glory of God to return to the temple, for God's favor to again come. The court crier, the announcer of Jesus' divine kingship, was not a Hebrew prophet, nor a respected rabbi. Shockingly, he was a Roman centurion. "Surely this man was the Son of God!" (Mark 15:39 NIV). Something deeper was at play. The great centrifugal force of God's purpose was breaking into history. Of all the people to announce the King, it was a cog in the Roman military machine. The war against flesh had been turned on its head.

Jesus put flesh to death in sweeping measure. Our individual sin and rebellion; our fleshly structures and systems, corporately erected to protect us from the flesh yet enslaving us to that very flesh; our attempts at reentering the holy space on our own strength—He took all of it upon Himself. He made a royal mockery of it and left it dead outside the Holy City. Jesus' answer to the flesh wasn't to restrain it, but to slaughter it.

Having defeated sin upon the cross, Jesus emerged from the grave. Human flesh, body, and bone, but transformed. The future of humanity for those who bend their knee to Christ, on display in a human being. The miracle of the resurrection was not just a once-off, individual miracle reserved for the risen Christ. It was and is an invitation to join God's salvation project, to be resurrected, to live fully human lives through the work of Jesus, minus the corruption of the flesh.

IN-BETWEEN DAYS

As the implications of Jesus' atoning death and resurrection swirled in the social firmament, strange gatherings happened across the Roman world. Jews, Gentiles, slaves, free people, men, and women met together, laying down their statuses and identities and bowing knees—not before the emperor, but a Galilean Jew they claimed had risen from the grave. Off the radar, something radical, something momentous, had occurred. The church had been born. Gentiles no longer plotting with their brothers in vain, nor Jews living out of the Torah, which protected against the flesh but could not save from it. Instead a new kind of life, a life in the Spirit, had begun—a following of Jesus' example of living in the flesh but not being controlled by the flesh, instead abiding in the Father, living by the power and direction of the Spirit.

The nations had rebelled and conspired against God and harassed the people of God. Now, however, following the atoning death of Christ, the church, those living out this new life in the Spirit, was sent out to the nations. Jesus charged His disciples to go into the nations, baptizing them, making them disciples of Christ. Redemption would come to the nations. They would, as the prophets had promised, recognize God as king, and this redemption would come through a transformed people, a church of disciples, fighting the flesh and living through the Spirit. The world had entered a new epoch.

PART 2

HISTORICAL PATTERN OF CHAOS

CHAPTER THREE

THE RELIGIOUS ARCHITECTURE OF EVERY SOCIETY

No secular society exists or has ever existed. However religion is defined, all institutions, structures, and patterns of behavior have religious features. All cultures are infused with values and actions that have religious dimensions and overtones. Whether they name the name of a known god or not, societies and cultures are always patterned by some ultimate inspiration and aspiration."[1] So writes Peter Leithart in *Elements of the World.* What he says here introduces a fundamental principle for moving ahead. Humans are not just social creatures, but religious ones, too. The root of the word "culture" is *cultus*, a Latin word meaning "to care, or tend a sacred site of worship." Culture is an expression of worship. For contemporary Westerners attuned to the idea that faith is a private belief in a supernatural being, this can be a new and jarring thought. We may see ourselves as thoroughly secular, but our lives and societies are contoured to religion. The complexities of the world, so often seemingly random, become clearer when we understand the religious impulses behind our social architecture.

Leithart notes that behind all social architecture, be it ancient or modern, Western or non-Western, are "practices concerning holiness, purity, and sacrifice."[2] These are the rules, rituals, relationships, and social structures that organize life. They are arranged around concepts of who is in and who is out (borders); what makes a person, place, or thing pure and safe (purity); and what practices defend the purity of a border against what is dangerous, unclean, and unholy (sacrifice).

We see the elements of borders, purity, and sacrifice throughout the story of Omar Mateen's attack on the Pulse nightclub in Florida.

In a painfully awkward interview following the shooting, CNN host Anderson Cooper confronted conservative Attorney General of Florida Pam Bondi with the fact that he had searched through her history of tweets, and that she had not shown enough historical support of the LGBT community. This accusation seemed to capture a mood among many progressives, born of the belief that Omar Mateen's actions were not primarily an act of ISIS-inspired terrorism but due rather to a broader atmosphere of homophobia. A protest in the wake of the shootings was fronted by a banner proclaiming that fault for the shooting lay with Republicans. We can see in the progressive response to radical Islam a desire to find the real source of evil, locating it not in radical Islam but rather the looming pollution of homegrown bigotry. Another manifestation of the religious elements, a desire to see borders of the West purified from the pollutant of discrimination.

Additionally, after the attack calls came in for tighter controls on Muslim immigration or even a total ban. In response to Islamic migration and terrorist attacks in the West, especially following the migrant crisis, government officials have been pressured to give greater acknowledgment to the threat of Islamic radicalism. Others have lobbied governments that the Judeo-Christian roots of Western society be preserved in the face of growing Islamic minorities. That concrete action beyond simple law enforcement be taken to contain the threat, which had taken on the form of a cultural battle between the Christian West and Islam. Ignoring the fact that most ISIS-inspired attacks in the West were committed by lone wolves born in the West, seduced by online propaganda, the belief was that this contagion could be kept at bay by strengthening borders and boundaries, by keeping the infection out. The enemy was "out there," not inside. *The danger was conveyed as an existential threat to the West itself.* The West, in such a response, is imagined as a kind of sacred space. In this response we see the elemental building blocks at play, the concept of a pure space, of purification, of sacrifice.

But it's not just Western Christians who seek to defend their space. Undoubtedly, the Pulse nightclub was attacked because it was a gay nightclub, and ISIS, alongside radical jihadists, sees homosexuality as a capital offense. But read ISIS and jihadi statements, justifications and press releases, and you see that Islamic terrorists have an incredibly broad definition of immorality. They are offended by homosexual acts, but also by intermingling of the sexes, dancing, photographs of humans, alcohol, cigarettes, and trouser cuffs that touch the ground.

Mateen's original target was Disney World, abandoned because of its tight security. ISIS's justification for targeting its Paris attacks at The Eagles of Death Metal concert at the Bataclan theater was not that it wanted to attack people having fun, but rather that it was a den of prostitution in need of purification. In Turkey, radical Islamists attacked a gathering of bookish hipsters enjoying a listening party for the new Radiohead album because they say it is immoral. Ironically, many fans interpreted the lyrics of the lead single, "Burn the Witch," as a commentary against the growing groupthink and authoritarianism in the world, the desire to protect communities from the threat of the "outsider."

The idea that progressives, vehemently opposed to those who hold to a traditional view of sexuality and family life, would appear to offer apology for radical Islam would be too much for some. This mood would intersect with the sentiment established by the New Atheism of Richard Dawkins and Christopher Hitchins in the wake of the 9/11 attacks—that the truest threat to the West's liberal tolerant society was the intolerance of religions, most notably in the form of Islam. In other words, religion is the culprit.

In Europe this mood has been fermenting for some time. European far-right figures such as Geert Wilders and Marine Le Pen publicize themselves as defenders of women and the LGBT community against the dangers of immigration and Islam. Some European countries, opposed to physical walls on their borders, instead proposed erecting cultural boundaries, showing potential migrants images and videos of men kissing, or women bathing topless, to communicate they'd feel out of place in Europe.

In this configuration of the religious elements, the most important line between insider and outsider falls not between Muslim and Christian, or theist and atheist, but adherence to the dogma of Western sexual freedom.

So you see that not just the West but indeed the world is becoming a construction site where walls—physical, cultural, and spiritual—are being simultaneously erected and torn down. All in an effort to keep the chaos at bay, to reach for the purity of a utopia, to find a sense of home, and security. A map is emerging, a compass with which to navigate the complexities of our world. "Locate the sacred center of a group; its boundaries of tolerable and intolerable persons, objects and behavior; its rituals of sacrifice—discover all this and you have got down to the elementary particles."[3]

SACRED BOUNDARIES

PURITY

SACRIFICES

Humans are God-centered creatures; even when we run from Him we still create religious systems and structures. The world, our cultures, is crisscrossed with religious lines.

GLOBALIZATION

Because of our flesh, our mortality, and our human condition, our boundaries are important. They are imbued with deep, transcendent meaning, guiding beyond the individual to a greater truth. They offer means of understanding the world and processing our experiences. They are beacons of guidance.

So when boundaries are moved, reimagined, made porous, or disappear, confusion and conflict are introduced, and anxiety arises. "All margins are dangerous. If they are pulled this way or that the shape of fundamental experience is altered. Any structure of ideas is vulnerable at its margins,"[4] writes anthropologist Mary Douglas. For example South Africa, during white rule, was isolated from the world, cut off by sanctions and international condemnation. However, in post-apartheid South Africa, connected again to the global economy, a recent spate of racist attacks against migrants has been perpetrated by those who only a few decades ago suffered under the racist apartheid policy. Those who felt a sense of solidarity in suffering now respond to the porousness of their own borders with anxiety, prejudice, and fear of the outsider. The victims of racism, becoming perpetrators.

Globalization feels like a threat because it disrupts our boundaries. It upsets our equilibrium. This is the tension the world is feeling. Benjamin Barber, in *Jihad vs. McWorld,* says globalization makes the world seem as if it is "falling precipitously apart and coming reluctantly together at the very same moment."[5] It makes everywhere seem like everywhere else. Thomas Friedman, in *The Lexus and the Olive Tree,* similarly defines globalization as "the inexorable integration of markets, nation-states and technologies to a degree never witnessed before—in a way that is enabling individuals, corporations, and nation-states to reach around the world farther, faster, deeper, cheaper than ever before."[6] Globalization integrates cultures, expanding our ability to reach around the world and move across boundaries. For traditional societies, meaning is found in the correct and sacred ordering of space and time. Globalization radically rearranges both.[7]

Consider the effects of globalization on our familiar places, for example. Increasingly we find the same stores, food, fashions, and lifestyles in the world's major cities. So it can seem like cultures are losing their cohesion and uniqueness. Our familiar markers, rituals, and traditions are changing, bringing anxiety. A letter to the editor in my local paper today is a prime example. An older resident of my neighborhood, lamenting the incredible changes in the area of the last year. The streets that were once quiet and community minded, now punctured with growing skyscrapers, built for short-term leasers and foreign students, funded by overseas investment. The demolishment of vintage homes and local landmarks by foreign investors. The lightning-quick demographic shift, from a family area to a predominantly mainland Chinese population, of short term renters, and overseas students. The letter filled with a mourning, a culture shock, a lament at a lost sense of community, of "home" disappearing. Such senses of loss and displacement drive some to religion, but they also fuel and are exploited by populist parties on the far reaches of the right and left. Because they involve a deep sense of home, a spiritual hole, they create in us religious responses. Through globalization, the world—both good and bad—is brought close, and boundaries lose their integrity. The trajectory of globalism crosses borders, reconfiguring or even eliminating them. Our sense of having a place—be it home, motherland, tribe, or people—is weakened or even destroyed.

Even the socioeconomic dynamics of globalization—specifically global capitalism and the Internet—work against the maintenance of place, boundaries, and borders. For some, globalization brings not wealth but the displacement of poverty. Farmers flee to the city to find work. The economic forces of globalization create a new class of jet-setters but also economic refugees. Globalization creates winners and losers, and the losers often lose their sense of home. Friedman notes that the effects of globalization are "producing a powerful backlash from those brutalized or left behind by this new system."[8] Whole industries can be moved to foreign locales, in order to benefit from cheaper overheads and a lower wages. Entire towns, cities, and regions, built around certain industries, in particular manufacturing, can be devastated overnight.

There is even a spiritual application to Friedman's observation. The boundary-eliminating momentum of globalization can push us into spiritual poverty, as the markers that illuminated and protected great meanings disappear. This process leaves many disoriented and directionless, looking for ways of remarking the borders and boundaries. They become spiritually *placeless* because the *boundaries of locations sacred and pure to them are punctured, crossed, or abused.* Western secularism likes to imagine that religion can be relegated to the private sphere, an internalized personal faith that is easily transported, and malleable. However, as we have discovered, faith, culture, and society are deeply connected. Religion is not as flexible as those who do not really believe in it imagine.

And so, whether it affects spatial, cultural, economic, or spiritual familiarity, globalization can feel like one big disruption, rattling the core of who we are. You can imagine it like this:

As globalization stretches our borders, erases meanings and traditions, and our concepts of place are renegotiated, possibilities and problems emerge. Migrants can, in a new land or city, seek out religious communities, often initially for practical purposes. Faith can be found or deepened. Religious community strengthened. Belief revived and passed through an international chain of relationships. At the same time however, as frustrations grow, religion and culture can retreat, violently lashing out at dominant cultures, seeing them as enemies intent on overrunning everything that is sacred. As one migrant character in Zadie Smith's novel *White Teeth* notes, the fear that locals sometimes have of their culture being erased by migrants is nothing compared to the fear the migrant has that their own

culture will be decimated by the new culture they find themselves in. Culturally and religiously disoriented, more radical
and dangerous forms of religion, ideology, and nationalism
can take hold; for example, more terrorist attacks per capita
are committed by Belgian Muslims from Brussels, than most
Muslim nations.[9]

Rapid cultural dislocation can create a powder keg. However,
it is important to note that the proponents of globalization are
not just advocates for an economic order, which connects the
world through trade and migration, but also of the belief that
globalization's erasing of borders, place, and local meanings is
essential for humankind's development. This belief runs deep in
the Western imagination, still driving much of the ideological
force of globalization. It is to this history we must turn next.

CHAPTER 4

CIVILIZATIONS STRIVING

Are you looking for freedom?" sang the large American wearing a mullet and flashing lights. David Hasselhoff had chosen his outfit so the crowd in the Berlin square could see him. It was New Year's Eve, 1989. Several weeks earlier the boundary dividing East and West Germany had fallen. Hasselhoff's single "Looking for Freedom" had been adopted as an anthem for the nation now seeking reunification, becoming a #1 hit in Europe's German-speaking nations. While statues of Marx and Lenin fell across the communist world, Hasselhoff stood atop the Berlin Wall as a kind of flesh statue of globalization. Soon he would emerge an icon of utopia, a beach-body god of American freedom. As he finished his performance, still feeding off the energy of the crowd, Hasselhoff *whooped*, giddy with exhilaration. This euphoria would be felt across the world as midnight fell and the eighties—a decade of tension and terror—turned into the nineties.

The doomsday clock, a tool scientists used to illustrate how close the world was to nuclear Armageddon, had been wound back. As the final decade of the twentieth century began, a century marked by two devastating World Wars and the struggle of the Cold War, hope arose. A new millennium was dawning. The rapid fall of communism caught a whole generation of Western diplomats and politicians off guard.

The word *history* was on everyone's tongue. The reformist Soviet leader Mikhail Gorbachev declared, "To oppose freedom of choice means placing oneself against the objective movement of history itself."[1] Bob Gates, former director of the CIA, saw the moment as an unstoppable force, noting that his agency "had no idea in January 1989 that a tidal wave of history was about to break upon us."[2] Musing on the changes in the world, the British band Jesus Jones penned a worldwide hit, singing, "Right here, right now, there is no other place I wanna be / Right here, right now, watching the world wake up from history."[3]

Every epoch of history has been marked by struggle, chaos, and wars. Yet part of the reason we feel as if we're living in strange days, like culture is decaying and the world is moving into greater conflict, is because of a fundamental and implicit assumption. The assumption is that we have reached a new era of human history, a post-conflict world in which we'll gently slide toward a future both diverse and tolerant, a tomorrow in which cooperation, technology, and globalization will lead the world into a new and wonderful present. Undergirding this assumption is a strange belief that goes back to the eighteenth century.

OPTIMISM SURGES, WANES, AND RISES AGAIN

The Enlightenment, a philosophical movement that emerged in Europe in the eighteenth century, believed advances in scientific knowledge and exploration would bring a brighter human future, that human hands alone could fashion the social dimension of the kingdom of God. As Catholic historian Christopher Dawson wrote, the thinkers of the Enlightenment had "an optimistic faith in the abrupt advent of a new age of justice and enlightenment, in which their most extravagant hopes for the future of humanity would be realised."[4] The abruptness of this historical change emerged from the rejection—a firm rejection—of human imperfection. "Belief in progress would often be more correctly described as the belief in human perfectibility."

The philosopher Immanuel Kant, a humanist and major figure of the Enlightment, dreamed of a community of nations that would adhere to global laws, with this international cooperation leading to a new golden period on earth of perpetual peace.

However, this faith would be jolted by the catastrophic conflict of World War I, as Europe's self-imagined progressive nations would find themselves drowning in a sea of mud and blood. Instead of progressing to a peaceful global future, fascism wished to return to the past of land, tribe, blood, and community—seemingly innocuous words, but holding deeply racist meanings in the fascist imagination. Soon these forces would unleash World War II, a second devastating blow against the West. After millions of deaths, after Hiroshima and the Nazi death camps, and as the ice of the Cold War set in, it was impossible to ignore the dark potential of human nature.

The Cold War was a conflict shadowed by the fear of nuclear Armageddon, which carried the potential to wash away the fruits of liberal democracy and return the West to a Mad Max, post-apocalyptic existence. People expected the final showdown to happen in Berlin, where the wall represented two opposing forces: communism and liberal democracy. The West saw itself in West Berlin—a purified space of the sacred values of personal liberty, equality, and democracy—but isolated and surrounded by dangerous, aggressive forces.

Outside of the West, this view of the world as a dangerous place persisted even as the Berlin Wall fell and communism ended. As the wall began to be torn down on November 9, another man the same age as Hasselhoff was frantically dialing the telephone. Whereas Hasselhoff's tall frame, confidence, and celebrity stylings ensured that he would stand out from the crowd, Vladimir Putin was short, with a nondescript manner, perfect for a KGB operative not wanting attention. As order began to break down in East Germany, Putin holed up in the Berlin KGB headquarters, calling a nearby Soviet tank base for support. Moments earlier he had warned gathering protestors outside that he and his KGB comrades were armed. When uprisings like this had occurred in Hungary in 1956 and Prague in 1968, Moscow had sent in the tanks.

The word came back: "We cannot do anything without orders from Moscow. And Moscow is silent."[5] It was a defining moment for Putin. A confirmation that the world would not progress to a utopia, but rather was a dangerous place, of swirling, competing powers. For Russians, the post–Cold War era of the nineties was not an age of optimism, but rather a time of chaos and gangster capitalism. Journalist Ben Judah writes, "Putin's generation have been called 'generation emptiness.' They are men shaped by a tsunami of shopping, PR and state collapse, their thinking warped by post-modern philosophy amid ideological bankruptcy. It is a generation for whom too many have lost their ability to see right from wrong, and with it went all their certainties apart from cynicism."[6]

In contrast to this cynicism, the West was recharged by a bursting optimism. Francis Fukuyama, in his 1989 article "The End of History and the Last Man," optimistically argued that when the wall fell, history had come to an end—not in the sense of events ending, but that the promised communist utopia would never arrive, and that liberal democracies with free markets marked the end of humanity's struggle for the best form of social organization. The great ideological struggle that had defined the Cold War was over. The article was expanded into a bestselling book, catapulting Fukuyama into fame as an interpreter of the turn of history.

Fukuyama's essential argument was that history was the drama of humans seeking recognition of their inherent dignity. Humans' need to be recognized by others drove conflict, wars, and slavery. This desire for recognition was irrational. For human survival was not dependent upon it, yet we desired it. Following the thought of Hegel and Kojève, Fukuyama writes,

> Human beings like animals have natural needs and de-
> sires for objects outside themselves such as food, drink,
> shelter, and above all the preservation of their own
> bodies. Man differs fundamentally from the animals,
> however, because in addition he desires the desire

of other men, that is, he wants to be "recognized." In particular, he wants to be recognized as a *human being*, that is, as a being with a certain worth or dignity. This worth in the first instance is related to his willingness to risk his life in a struggle over pure prestige.[7]

Fukuyama's argument that liberal democracies, built on free-market economics (which enabled the pursuit of desires), democracy, rights, and representation (which provided humans with the recognition of their worth and dignity), were the signs that liberal democracies were the form of society that would leave people "completely satisfied."

Fukuyama's argument proved to be intoxicating as the world woke not to a bipolar globe split between the West and communism, but a unipolar globe, with America as the sole standing superpower. We were not on the verge of cultural decay, or Armageddon, but instead civilizational triumph. There were still some kinks to iron out, but the matter was settled; history was over. After the winter of the Cold War, a new summer seemed to be emerging.

DARK CLOUDS ON THE HORIZON

And so we come back to Hasselhoff. The world is breathing a collective sigh of relief that the wars are over and better days are ahead. Optimism is in the air and the blood. Understanding this is essential to understanding our current moment of anxiety. The post–Cold War era was a time of inflated expectations both on a corporate and individual level.

The society-wide utopian vision was almost invisible, for the utopia was a place in which individuals could reinvent themselves, find historically previously unknown freedoms, and look forward to an endless horizon as the stock market continued to climb. Consumerism had long shaped existence in the West, yet it took on a new power during this time, seemingly expanding the possibilities of a human life. Wants became muddled with needs. Desires supplanted duties. Celebrity culture took hold in a deeper way.

The desire to break the third wall of screen and life was already latently there before the Internet delivered it globally. Consider the live drama of the O. J. Simpson murder drama, in which crowds on the LA freeway injected themselves as participants into the media event, harbingers of the immersive social media culture to come. The advent of the Internet seemed to promise an even richer hue to the post–Cold War golden age.

The utopia of globalization found at the end of history offered a limitless expanse of options. Instead of commonality undergirded by shared cultural norms, there was an endless choice fueled by the unchallenged ethic of tolerance. The self would stand unbridled by the other. Internet deliveries, downloadable music, cheap airline travel, foodie culture, all expanding not only the pantheon of consumer choice but also seemingly a confirmation of Fukuyama's prediction of the end of history as a time in which the individual found satisfaction.

The education revolution of self-esteem messaging introduced into schools, children's books and television, and colleges saw the emergence of a new generation who had been encouraged that they all could be anything they wanted to be, that suffering, restrictions, and barriers could be overcome with self-confidence and pluck. Eventually, this self-belief in possibility would manifest itself in a winning presidential campaign slogan, "Yes We Can."

Emerging adulthood, rather than the teen years, midlife, or older years, became the cultural standard, as the delaying of childbirth, family, and marriage became the norm. Emerging adulthood is a time when *"no dreams have been permanently dashed, no doors have been permanently closed, every possibility for happiness is still alive"*[8] (emphasis mine). This sense of the possibility of individual dreams coming true broke out of the generation of emerging young adults and became a social mantra. Psychologist Jean Twenge notes that studies began to show that a majority of young adults believed that something truly magnificent was going to happen to them.[9]

Marketers, with their keen sense of what motivates us, powerfully set the expectations of a culture in which beautiful things were going to continue. Globalization appeared to be a reduction of the world into a blank canvas on which the individual could paint their dreams. Hubris, the sin of overconfidence and skyrocketing pride, once reserved as a moniker for flawed heroes in Greek mythology and decadent Roman emperors, began to shape the expectations and self-understanding of an entire generation—"millennials," we've called them. Beneath the surface, however, cracks were forming.

If narcissism, entitlement, and hubris defined the mid-2000s, it also defined the global financial crisis. The Greeks taught that nemesis always follows hubris. The downfall of the global financial system began a series of shocks, each denting the individualized Western bubbles filled with expectation. The initial shock of the financial crisis and the ongoing slog of the war on terror seemed for a moment to be outshone, as Barack Obama, draped in his slogan of "Hope," appeared before crowds in Millennium Park, Chicago. As tears of optimism fell, the atmosphere seemed to many like the beginning of a new epoch, a post-racial era, an age of civilized democracy.

As those on the left lauded, and those on the right fumed, both made the error of assuming that the most powerful office in the world could control the forces at play in the world. What was occurring was not a diminishment of American hard or soft power, but the emergence of the swirling force of a hyperconnected and chaotic world—globalization. The shocks kept coming.

The effects of the global financial crisis took hold, and dictatorships of the Middle East turned into dystopias. Al-Qaeda, which shocked the world on 9/11, would soon be disgusted by the barbarism of their offspring, ISIS, against whom they would declare war. Flashpoints would emerge across the globe, as between 2008–2016 the individualized bubbles of entitlement and expectation would stretch to breaking point. As Robert Kagan writes:

> The years immediately following the end of the Cold War offered a tantalizing glimpse of a new kind of international order, with nation-states growing together or disappearing altogether, ideological conflicts melting away, cultures intermingling, and increasingly free commerce and communications. The modern democratic world wanted to believe that the end of the Cold War did not just end one strategic and ideological

conflict but all strategic and ideological conflict. But that was a mirage. The world has not been transformed. In most places, the nation-state remains as strong as ever, and so, too the nationalist ambitions, the passions, and the competitions among nations that have shaped history.[10]

For Kagan and others skeptical of the thesis that the world had reached a post-conflict age, *the world had become normal again.* According to Robert D. Kaplan, the mirage of the end of conflict and struggle, of the West's ability to remake the world, was one maintained by the power of its military, which simply held the submerged forces of conflict at bay.[11] The tolerant culture of progressive equality was held in place by tanks and cruise missiles. History had not ended; the great forces that caused the nations to buck against their chains were always there, we just chose to look away.

* * * * *

The reason we feel as anxious as we do is that we don't see what we expected. We came running into the new world with arms raised in triumph, like a boxer waiting for flowers to flood the ring. But as the darkness swirls around us, our posture shifts. Our arms slouch in confusion, as if to ask, "What is this?" Expect utopia, and dystopia is jarring.

CHAPTER 5

NON-PLACES, PRAYER CLOSETS OF INDIVIDUALISM

In Tom McCarthy's 2015 novel *Satin Island,* the protagonist, simply know as U., is tasked by a multinational company to compile "the great report," a document that captures the contemporary global moment. As an anthropologist, someone who studies people and cultures in their native lands, U. spends his time flying across the world, observing, recording, and chasing down leads, hunting meaning in a web of complexity. But he wishes to be an anthropologist of the contemporary, not observing and recording far away cultures, but the global culture in which he lives.

However, the task of capturing the current cultural mood becomes near impossible, as culture is in constant flux, its expanding complexity beyond grasp. As U. waits for a flight, he begins to see the hub airport as symbolic of our contemporary epoch, not a destination but a transfer place, constantly in flux. As he waits, his phone buzzes with text messages in his pocket from his boss, and he speaks to his girlfriend on Skype while simultaneously surfing the Internet, blurring the line between field and home, observer and observed.

All around him are fragments of sound, the whoosh of steam from espresso machines, spurts of music and conversation. The television screens in the lounge broadcast a football match, a market bombing, and an oil spill disaster. The images reflect off onto the smooth surfaces of the nearby luxury stores, creating a collage of the carnage of the terrorist bombing and devastation of the oil spill mixing with objects of desire of the global elites. The complexity, the flux, the atmospherics of the hub airport creates in U. a feeling of *"vertigo tinged with a slight nausea ... an awkward sense of things being out of sync, out of whack"*[1] (emphasis mine).

It's no accident that U. is called U., for we are all U., all trying to interpret our world and mine it for meaning. But we are overwhelmed with the sheer volume of options and information, struggling to keep our head above the waters of superabundance. This chapter is about a common effort to stay afloat: retreating to "non-places." We'll see that the effort is not only counterproductive, but also forms our identities in such a way that we hamstring ourselves in our pursuit of human flourishing.

LIVING IN NON-PLACES

According to anthropologist Marc Auge, places are concerned with history, relationships, and identity. Someone can call a place "home," for example, or they can walk into it with a sense of belonging—like a workplace, church building, or relative's

home. Spaces that are *not* concerned with history, relationships, or identity, then, are *non-places*.

For Auge, hotels, airports, and highways are examples of
non-places. There is no shared identity there, no story in the
soil, no legends of a people or group. They are not places for
setting down roots, but instead are built for rootlessness, for
passing through. You might be relational there, but usually to
an absolute minimum. The superficial pleasantries of a hotel
check-in or having your name called at a chain coffee shop—
these are more about functionality than relationship. They are
interactions of commercial contractualism.

Whereas place gives identity, the non-place offers only
tips and lifestyle advice with which to shape one's identity.
Advertisements, celebrities, and the educational process of
the lifestyle industry provide aspirational role models, which,
in Auge's words, "enable individuals subjected to the global
constraints of modern—especially urban—society to deflect
them, to make use of them, to contrive through a sort of everyday tinkering to establish their own decor and trace their own
personal itineraries."[2] The non-place is place reduced for max-
imum individual freedom, shorn of the restrictions of binding
relationships, externally given identities, and the responsibility
of history.

Relationships, identity, and history are three elements that
contribute to the meaning-making function of "place." Traditionally, in almost all human societies, individuals find meaning
in the grid of relationships into which they are born and within
which they exist throughout their life. This dense web of relationships gives one a sense of community and belonging. The

cost of such a relational network is *commitment*; one is bound through loyalty to those around them, which ensures that the strength of community can continue to offer meaning and belonging. However, in contemporary Western culture, this dense web of relationships has slowly eroded, worn away by radical individualism, contemporary mobility, and an approach to relationships shaped by shopping and consumerism. We fear commitment and don't want to be bound, preferring instead to travel relationally light. Thus we have more freedom, but the cost is a sense of lostness, isolation, and an absence of meaning. The non-place is defined by this light approach to relationships, built around individual freedom and movement.

Throughout human history identity, too, has been something externally conferred. The dense web of relationships gives meaning through conferring markers of identity upon the individual. That is, we are known through and defined by our close connections. However, as contemporary Western thought favors the authority of the individual over the collective, it is the individual who gets to create his or her identity. Our search for freedom is also perceived as the freedom to define, and even continually redefine, one's identity as he or she wishes. The non-place, unlike the place, does not tell us who we are. Identity is reduced to the barest markers, such as the details upon one's boarding pass, which allows entry to the airport gate, or the credit card number, which allows one to shop online.

Not only do non-places detach us from relationships and identity, they also remove a sense of history. The long line of our descendants who go before us, and who will go ahead of many of us, has been seen throughout history as a key element in informing who we are. The places and events that we, our relatives, and our community have known and experienced are a definitive marker of who we are. However, the non-place is largely detached from history. Yesterday I was recounting the story to my wife of an ill young man I had seen at an airport food court. She asked which airport it had been. I could not recall; I was unable to even remember what country or continent I had been in, due to the lack of historical markers to place and people.

In the global utopia imagined after the Cold War, the world would be a kind of non-place, a fenceless field in which individuals could pursue their dreams and flourish without restrictions. You can draw out the concept of non-places like so:

NON-PLACE

no-history
no-relationships
no-identity

COCOONING IN THE CHAOS

Remembering what we discussed last chapter—the tension between the utopia we expected and the chaos we experience gives us a profound sense of dislocation—helps us understand our increased draw to non-places. They are neutral ground, ideal "places" for retreating. They are closets where we can shut the door, turn off the lights, and hide. In a chaotic world, this kind of cocooning is the new social reflex.

But our cocoons are not incidental. As I said earlier, the medium holds meaning. If we escape to books or the woods, for example, our experience of the world would be vastly different than if we escape to technology, which we often do, because it's the most accessible, and least demanding, escape. The increasing sophistication of consumerism, the rise of the Internet, and in particular the rise of smartphones offers us a convenient and even gratifying life-world, a non-place where we can relax and yet stay in control—a seemingly ideal way to indulge the end-of-history dream at a personal level. The non-place has shrunk from the scale of an airport lounge or a mall to the size of a screen that fits in your palm, allowing you to escape into it at any time, to retreat from place to non-place at your desire.

The non-places of our world, embassies of globalization, appear to be an escape from the controversies of religion and ideology. However, recovering from, and reflecting upon, the cost of living in the non-place that is the Internet, ex-blogger Andrew Sullivan encourages us to see this change:

> Just look around you—at the people crouched over their phones as they walk the streets, or drive their cars, or walk their dogs, or play with their children. Observe yourself in line for coffee, or in a quick work break, or driving, or even just going to the bathroom. Visit an airport and see the sea of craned necks and dead eyes. We have gone from looking up and around to constantly looking down. If an alien had visited America just five years ago, then returned today,

wouldn't this be its immediate observation? That this species has developed an extraordinary new habit—and, everywhere you look, lives constantly in its thrall?[3]

The draw to non-places is to find freedom, but does anyone actually experience them that way? The non-places of globalization, be they a multinational clothing store, an exurb filled with neighbors who never speak to each other, or our smartphones, are far from neutral, ideology-free zones. They have an agenda. They are designed to illicit a particular response within you. Malls are designed to disorientate you in a phenomenon known as the "Gruen transfer," leading you into stores and selling points you never intended to enter. We have all experienced this phenomenon, ducking into the store to grab a handful of groceries but emerging with a new pair of sneakers or an electronic gadget. This phenomenon does more than simply make us buy items we do not need; it creates a kind of person, one docile and easily manipulated, individualistic and confused about their identity, thus looking for products and experiences that will fulfill our desire for meaning and identity. As psychologist Dan Ariely writes, "The world is not acting in our long-term benefit. Imagine you walk down the street and every store is trying to get your money right now; in your pocket you have a phone, and every app wants to control your attention right now. Most of the entities in our lives really want us to make mistakes in their favor. So the world is making things very, very difficult."[4] We wrap ourselves in our lounge rooms and flat-screen televisions for safety, but the irony is that it is in these very places we are bombarded with chaos. The screens we escape to to binge on the latest HBO series are the same ones that deliver live footage of the unfolding terrorist attack. Our cocooning and escapism is achieved via the same medium that brings us unprecedented access to a flood of information about a world in chaos.

FORMED BY OUR PHONES

Dwelling in non-places does more than just add to our sense of chaos, however. Non-places are also formative. They are more than closets; they are *prayer* closets, filled with what James K. A. Smith calls *secular liturgies*. Liturgies, whether religious or secular, "shape and constitute our identities by forming our most fundamental desires and our most basic attunement to the world. In short, liturgies make us certain kinds of people, and what defines us is what we love."[5] *The key point here is that it is what we do rather than what we believe that ultimately shapes us.* Few parents wish not to be present with their children, yet just observe the contemporary parents with their children at the park, lost in their phones, while their children attempt to gain their attention. It is as Aristotle once remarked, *we are what we repeatedly do.*

Smith writes, "Every liturgy constitutes a pedagogy that teaches us, in all sorts of precognitive ways, to be a certain kind of person. Hence every liturgy is an education, and embedded in every liturgy is an implicit worldview or 'understanding' of the world."[6] The education of non-places is built on the idea that the world should be a comfortable space for us to pursue our pleasures and individual agendas. Whether we are atheist, Christian, Jew, Hindu or agnostic, the secular liturgy of the non-places of globalization shapes us to view the world in its particular way, to see creation as a kind of personal playground.

Ultimately, non-places communicate the myth that a particular kind of life is possible—a detached, free-floating life bereft of responsibility, in which one can walk through the rainstorm and stay dry, avoiding the difficulties, blockages, and restrictions humans have always encountered. Our non-place habits are liturgies that shape us, fool us, into thinking we can have total freedom, expanding human flourishing, and satisfaction through the consumption of products and experiences. They whisper to us that we can be godlike, hovering above it all while maintaining individual autonomy.

Non-places are the nexus point where a number of strands of contemporary Western culture come together. The dogma that life is all about feeling good and the inflation of self-esteem. The creed of consumerism, in which we construct identity and meaning through spending. The myth of radical individualism, in which we can flourish purely by pursuing our own personal agenda. They subtly yet radically inflate our expectations of what the good life is, pumping up our sense of self—but into an ugly shape that inevitably pops.

By their sealed nature, the security at the doors, the ambient music softly playing in the background, the minimalist modern design, non-places attempt to convince us that the problems of the world, the raging of the nations, the hurricane of sin, suffering, and evil, can be kept outside. They encourage us to not think about it, insist that you can be hermetically sealed from the fate of the world. Non-places are the temples of the West's religion, which masquerades as a non-religion. Preaching an oversimplification of life. Appearing to be content free while discipling us in a secular fundamentalism. The gospel that the world is your playground. Evangelizing us into a faith that fails.

ANXIOUS SMILES

At its core, however, world-as-playground is a myth, one that continues to come under increasing strain in the face of reality. A decade on from the optimism of the mid-2000s, potential, entitlement, and possibility were still in the air, but so was anxiety. And anxiety seemed to be winning. As the millennial emerging adults became simply adults, they faced the realities, disappointments, and difficulties adults have always encountered. The difference was that many were poorly prepared for this eventuality. This was not just true of millennials, but also for the optimistic age they embodied. The smile was there, but now it seemed strained.

Increasingly over the last five years, after I speak to larger groups, I am approached by people with virtually the same query. The people are different, and from various fields—businesspeople, principals, coaches, pastors—but they all lead younger adults who cannot cope any longer. They don't turn up to work for days, disappear from leadership positions, are exhausted but often appear to do little. They struggle with the most basic of tasks, yet wish for greater recognition, swinging from overconfidence to crippling insecurity. What puzzles these leaders is that such behavior would be understandable if the person had a history of tragedy, yet many of these people had come from stable families and privileged environments.

Maclean's magazine reported on the growing crisis, in colleges, of students feeling exhausted, depressed, anxious, and overwhelmed, noting that young adults "are having difficulty coping with the rapidly changing world around them, a world where they can't unplug, can't relax, and believe they must stay at the top of their class, no matter what."[7] The article noted that what is remarkable about this trend is that it is affecting those who are at the top of the social scale. Ivy League schools are struggling with an epidemic of mental health challenges. Prestigious Cornell College in Ithaca, New York, renowned for its beautiful grounds and picturesque bridges where students walk to class, now enclose those bridges in steel nets to arrest the spate of suicides.

This anxious mood is not just a millennial phenomenon. Parents of young kids are always tired, and there is nothing like the task of raising children filled with energy, needing discipline, care, and love. Sleeplessness and sickness have always been par for the course of parenting. However, now the task of parenting seems to come as a brutal shock, an assault upon comfort and personal liberty. Postnatal depression is often now affecting both mother and father. A growing fear affects those older as well, a sense that the world is awry, a job market that sees them as too old, a culture whose values they no longer understand, a world of technology rapidly moving ahead.

The role of parents has traditionally been to care and nurture, but also to educate the child in the tragic nature of life, the inevitability of suffering and mortality. The initiation ceremonies and rites of passage of many tribal groupings and cultures are a pedagogy in resetting one's expectations from the naïveté of childhood to the street smarts of adulthood. These countless cultures also knew the link between suffering and sanctity, between difficulty and the development of character. However, in the Western bubble of comfort, the role of parents and educators has been to protect first children, then teenagers, and then even young adults from the sting of suffering, tragedy, and even consequence—the traditional engines of character formation.

This kind of parenting and education is born of an extreme vision of the fragility of humans, a belief in the excessive damage done by exposure to suffering and hardship. Thus a damaging cocktail was prepared, a self-esteem message that inflated expectations beyond measure, which gave esteem disconnected from achievement. For many, the promise of the optimistic years of the early 2000s turned into a failure to launch, creating boomerang kids returning home and falling into underemployment. And those who do find work feel worked to the bone, like life is reduced to a never-ending burden of expectations.

Philosopher Byung-Chul Han notes that fatigue, anxiety, and attention deficit mark many today. We have moved from a disciplinary society, in which the social structure provides restraints, authority, and rules, to an achievement society. Whereas, according to Han, a disciplinary society is driven by the verb *should,* in which society asserts its force against the individual to move them in a socially acceptable direction, the achievement society is powered by the verb *can.* Instead of the negatives of the disciplinary society, the achievement society tells all that they can do it all, have it all, and be all. Han writes, "Contemporary society, however, is a society of achievement; increasingly, it is shedding the negativity of prohibitions and commandments and presenting itself as a society of freedom."[8]

The individual's challenge in the achievement society is to not be overrun by the excess of positivity. With the no-limits of non-places, individuals overwhelm themselves, struggling to meet their self-image and achieve their inflated expectations. In contrast to the disciplinary society, which erected barriers, rules, and taboos to maintain social cohesion with the other, in the achievement society, the other is nonexistent. Thus the self struggles to define the other. And God, as "the other" who offers guidance, authority, and moral limits, is dispensed. Without guidance, the self becomes anxious, agitated, and fearful, caught in a constant mood from which it cannot escape. The individual becomes his own judge. Holding his self-worth against the unrealistic expectations society has given him, he falls into tiredness and exhaustion. Instead of being exploited in the disciplinary society, in the achievement society the self exploits itself, becoming depressed. According to Han, this cycle

> often culminates in burnout—follows from overexcited, overdriven, excessive, self-reference that has assumed destructive traits. The exhausted, depressive achievement-subject grinds itself down, so to speak. It is tired, exhausted by itself, and at war with itself. Entirely incapable of stepping outward, of standing outside itself, of relying on the Other, on the world. It locks its jaws on itself; paradoxically, this leads the self to hollow and empty out. It wears out in a rat race it runs against itself.[9]

There is no rest for the weary in achievement society. The pace of life simply doesn't allow for recovery time. But taught to fear and flee from pain, suffering, and the negative, they become paralyzed, trapped between what they desire and their own limitations.

As the distance between expectations and reality grows, the individual will seek to control whatever he or she can, typically health and the body. Han observes, "The mania for health emerges when life has become as flat as a coin and stripped of all narrative content, all value. Given the atomization of society and the erosion of the social, all that remains is the body of the ego, which is to be kept healthy at any cost . . . Life reduced to bare, vital functioning is life to be kept healthy unconditionally. Health is the new goddess."[10] Ultimately, in the borderless freedom of the contemporary "non-place," individuals make their body a place, a sacred temple to be kept pure. Health becomes an obsession. The body another border. The self a secure land.

* * * * *

Our attempts to fight against change through protecting the boundaries of our sacred, purified non-places—through our screens, white ear buds, over-protective parenting, and trendy coffee shops—are failing us, fooling us with the belief that we can construct a protective bubble. Such a border attempts to keep the world's ills at bay, but it educates with a distorted view of the world, one that plunges us into a personal defeat.

So then, what do we make of non-places? We must recognize the irony of them. We are driven there by chaos, to shut out for a moment the fact that all is not right in the world. War, division, terrorism, ideological conflict—they make us afraid to go outside. So we retreat to our non-places. Yet what do we find there? An unending barrage of the very things we mean to escape. Further, the medium of our non-places forms in us a heightened sense of self. It feeds the ego to such a degree that we tower so tall above the other that we fail to even see them. This is isolation posing as power. The disconnection it breeds further reinforces our fear of the world, because inherent to fear is a lack of knowledge. Whatever the solution to the chaos all around us is, it cannot be the non-place. The non-place is invisible tundra, an expanse so utterly borderless and isolating that it may as well be solitary confinement.

CHAPTER 6

TERRORISM

It's morning and I am looking at my Twitter feed. A terrorist attack. As I get ready, and eat my breakfast, watching the feed for news, each fragment of information grows like a crystal. Tweets, shards of truth, floating speculations. An isolated loner? Another senseless massacre? The battle begins on Twitter. One team betting that it is an Islamic militant, hoping for confirmation of this fact to further underline the need to secure the borders, to confirm that the purity of the West is under threat from a religious ideology that wishes to do it harm. The other side claiming such speculation is racist and Islamaphobic and that the perpetrator is most likely a far-right-wing bigot.

The confirmation that the shooter was Muslim and had pledged allegiance to the Islamic state doesn't end the fiery debate. It goes on, the screens fill with experts, of differing political stripes and agendas, each offering clairvoyance into the shooter's motive. *Yet all missing the most obvious fact.*

Almost all Islamic terrorists leave behind detailed essays, statements, and suicide videos explaining their actions in detail.

We prefer to ignore this, for we must categorize their actions with our preexisting political and cultural frameworks. Force them into our political silos of left and right, bend them to fit into our Western cultural battles. Yet if we actually study their actions we see the underlying anthropological and religious components we discussed earlier: purity, boundaries, and sacrifice. Terrorism follows a religious sociology, one we can understand by traveling back to the origins of Islamic terrorism.

THE MESSIAH HAS COME BECAUSE OF TELEVISION

In November 1979 the Islamic world experienced its own version of 9/11 when jihadis seized the Grand Mosque in Mecca. It was the final day of the Hajj pilgrimage, and men were bowing for their morning prayers when wild-looking militants with long beards and rifles stormed in. Gunfire and cries of "Allahu Akbar" filled the sanctuary, sounds that would come to define the age of Jihadi terrorism. The chant alerted crowds that Mahdi, an Islamic messianic figure, was in their midst.

The attackers believed that the creeping influence of Western values in the kingdom is what precipitated the appearance of the Mahdi. Television had only recently appeared, but it was a powerful and seductive carrier of non-Islamic values. Additionally, global trade had brought a greater number of non-Islamic foreigners and Westerners onto the soil—a problem for those tasked with protecting the purity of Islam's holiest sites. Thus, according to Lawrence Wright, the militants used the Mosque as a sort of public address system to [insist] on the adoption of Islamic, non-Western values and the rupture of diplomatic relations with Western countries, thus rolling back the changes that had opened the society to modernity. The Saudi Arabia that these men wanted to create would be radically isolated ... Oil exports to the United States would be cut off, and all foreign civilian and military experts would be expelled from the Arabian Peninsula. The demands foreshadowed those that Osama bin Laden would make fifteen years later.[1]

In the view of the militants, the Islamic world lived in shame, spiritually polluted by foreign influences. Reestablishing a pure Mecca would be the starting point for a renewed and pure Islam.

The jihadi militants were descendants both biologically and theologically of the fierce Bedouin, shock troops the Saudi royal family used to carve out a nation on the Arabian peninsula. According to historian Robert Lacey, "Their imams had told them, in the historic tradition of Mohammed Ibn Abdul Wahhab ... that those who opposed them were *kuffar* (infidels), and thus deserving of death. They also believed that any *mujahid* (holy warrior) who died in battle would go straight to heaven."[2] For the desert followers of Wahhab, like their ideological descendants ISIS, the national borders drawn up following World War I were an abomination. For these nomadic tribesmen, only the religious borders and boundaries—the line between the infidels and the house of Islam—mattered.

FIGHTING WESTOXIFICATION

It is hard to overstate the distaste radical Islam has for Western values. The Iranian writer Jalal Al-e Ahmad coined the term *Westoxification* to describe the toxic cultural effect the West was having on the Middle East. He defines it as "the aggregate of events in the life, culture, civilization, and mode of thought of a people having no supporting tradition, no historical continuity, no gradient of transformation, but having only what the machine brings them."[3] Al-e Ahmad condemns the West as a non-place. The leader of the Iranian revolution, the Ayatollah Khomeini, rails against Westerners for their non-place ideology: "You, who want freedom, freedom for everything, the freedom of parties, you who want all the freedoms, you intellectuals: freedom that will corrupt our youth, freedom that will pave the way for the oppressor, freedom that will drag our nation to the bottom . . ."[4] If indeed Western ideologies are so corrupt and even threatening, then the natural response is, of course, to crush them.

Ironically, radical Islam would borrow a tactic from the West, from nineteenth-century leftist and anarchist radicals. Russian radical thinker Peter Kropotkin had a philosophy he labeled "the propaganda of the deed," which was the shocking use of violence to strike at the heart of an alluring culture of entertainment and materialism that threatened to seduce the working classes away from the revolution. Inspired by such a philosophy, Emile Henry, rootless and searching for meaning (much like Omar Mateen), would set off a bomb among the wine and song of the Cafe Terminus in Paris in 1884—killing one and wounding dozens. This seminal attack supports Marc

Auge's observation that terrorists usually attack non-places, like airports, cafés, and shopping malls.

Henry committed a sacrificial offering of the lives of the upwardly mobile. The radical anarchists, who were violently anti-Christian, nevertheless spoke of terrorism as a kind of sacrament. In fact, the anarchist-terrorist François Claudius Ravachol, who spent the last moments before his execution cursing Christ, was celebrated by the atheistic anarchists as a kind of martyr-christ, and his image was even made into radical icons.[5] The taking of life in order to reestablish the purity of the wished-for utopia—be it a workers' paradise or purified house of Islam—thus becomes not a murder, but a ritual, an act of worship.

In the mind of the militants, the modernizing, liberalizing impulse of globalization would be closed by this act of religious violence. A religious boundary would be reset, a clear border between profane and holy would be reimposed. The seizing of the Grand Mosque had created a nightmare of religious law for the Saudi government. As custodians of Islam's most sacred site, the eyes of the world's Muslims would be upon them, for the rules against violence in the Grand Mosque were crystal clear. The Saudi forces held back, while the religious deliberations began. The king turned to the council of religious clerics and scholars for clarification. Eventually, while the Islamic world held their breath, the council gave the king an emergency ruling, or fatwa, authorizing the Saudi forces to, in good religious faith, drive out the militants, who had holed themselves up in the mosque.

A series of foolhardy and costly assaults on the mosque,

done in desperation and fearing an utter bloodbath, led to a decision to use gas to overpower the jihadis. The surviving militants, their faces blackened and dirtied, were led out. Now the situation was reversed. Those who had taken up arms with the mission to purify the sanctity of Mecca, now looked, with their dirty faces and matted hair and beards, like pollutants, profaners of the holy sanctuary. In the world of religious boundaries, borders and taboos, the transgressor must face punishment. So the swords flashed, and heads rolled, as militants were sent out to the great frontier of death. However, for the jihadi cult, death was not an end; instead, it created martyrs, human sacrifices on the altar of purity.

GESTURING SYMBOLICALLY
TO A GLORIOUS PAST

Like the jihadis before him, Omar Mateen brandished an assault rifle and went about the work of purification, a deluded priestly figure committing a demented rite. Mateen, via Facebook and calls to 9-1-1, pledged allegiance to the Islamic State. His rampage was retaliation against the United States for bombing a mid-range ISIS leader—a fact that news anchors and politicized tweets threw around without an understanding of the attack's religious significance.

The Islamic State was far more than a state. It was a declared caliphate, "a concept freighted with huge religious and historical significance,"[6] say scholars Jessica Stern and J. M. Berger. ISIS's claim to the establishment of a caliphate in the summer of 2014 "gestures symbolically to a glorious past, it calls for allegiance . . . it explicitly rejects Western models of governance and secularism . . . it is unquestionably an attempt to return to an idealized form of government understood to have existed in an era when the Muslim world flourished,"[7] they write. Mateen's pledge of allegiance (or *bayah,* in Arabic) to the caliphate and its leader was a religious covenant binding him to the caliphate. It was simultaneously a rejection of a corrupted West and a declaration of the caliphate's religious and political utopia.

In mid-2014, ISIS—through a sophisticated and fruitful social media campaign—distributed a high-production video featuring a multicultural ensemble of Muslims from across the world who had made *hijrah,* or emigration, to the Islamic State. Fronted by an Islamic State foreign fighter from Finland, the video cuts to smiling children chanting:

> Our state was established upon Islam,
> And although it wages jihad against the enemies,
> It governs the affairs of the people.
> It looks after its flock with love and patience.
> The Shariah of our Lord is light, by it we rise over the stars.
> By it, we live without humiliation, a life of peace and security.[8]

The video is an example of the much-vaunted, skillful use of public relations and cutting-edge marketing by the Islamic State. Yet marketing and social media alone do not create movements, let alone ones that thousands of young people are inspired to cross continents to join and give their lives for in battle. Instead, the video shows that in our twenty-first century-globalized world, our desire for meaning, for place, for purpose, still burns deep. ISIS is not about the videos; it is about the dream of the caliphate.

A caliphate is a kind of earthly temple that offers a direct route to heaven for those who die defending its integrity. ISIS later declared that those who are unable to travel to the Islamic State should strike out against the infidel where they live, which is what Omar Mateen did. It is what numerous other young people have done across the world, as individuals or in groups. Attacks in Europe, Africa, North America, and Asia. A Brazilian ISIS-inspired cell arrested during the Olympics. Even the Caribbean island nation of Trinidad and Tobago is estimated to have as many of its citizens fighting for ISIS as the United States does.

As I write, only a few weeks ago in my home city of Melbourne, a Paris-style plot by a local cell to attack the downtown, and a Christmas Eve service at the city's main cathedral, was foiled by law enforcement. Immediately in the wake of the arrests of the plotters, again the usual talking points. The premier of the state announced that the attack had nothing to do with faith or religion, while others fumed that it had everything to do with the problem of radical Islam. Both sides failing to recognize that the modern war on terrorism is religious, not just the religion of radical jihadism; humans are religious creatures even as we attempt to flee religion. It is all religious.

CHAPTER 7

POLARIZED POLITICS

On February 28, 1972, the Japanese public was glued to its TV screens, entranced by a live broadcast. Police were laying siege to a lodge where a group of radical leftist students were killing each other.

Before I continue the story, it's important to give some background. The students had recently been sent into a crisis of doubt regarding communism due to its moral failures. When reports of genocide began surfacing—for example, that under Stalin nearly 100 million people had been killed—their confidence in communism, which had already been eroding, finally washed away. Faced with a crisis of identity, they clung to a different theory, one originally articulated by Alexandre Kojève.

This theory was called "The End of History," and we touched on it briefly in chapter 4. The idea is that the arrival of free, democratic, liberal societies signaled the highest peak of world culture. A society will flourish best when it can progress toward self-fulfillment without restriction. Equality, liberty, the absence of restrictive powers—these are essential ingredients for progressing toward utopia.

However, the group followed Kojève's thought to an extreme place. They saw the contemporary world as a giant, dehumanizing bureaucracy, one that controlled and repressed populations through cold science, rationality, and language. In this view almost every particle of contemporary Western culture was infused with micropowers, which maintained their hegemony by oppressing the other. Demons of oppression were found everywhere; evil was perceived as utterly rampant—education, history, politics, medicine, science, the family, gender, discourse, reason. Nuance was abandoned. The culture and society of the West was not a mixture of good and bad; rather it was all a sham, all evil, all an attempt to coerce and control. This stream of thought would come to be called the New Left.

Unlike the traditional leftists—who hoped, strived, and fought for the future utopia of communism, or the freedom of the working classes—for the New Left, if history had ended, there was little hope for change. All that one could do at the end of history was critique. Michel Foucault, a key thinker of the New Left, believed that critique should mean exposing of power. According to Roger Scruton, Foucault held that "behind every practice, every institution, and behind language itself [lay] power, and [Foucault's goal was] to unmask that power and thereby to liberate its victims."[1] Thus, according to this gospel, the salvation of humanity is found in the endless task of searching out and naming and shaming power where it can be found.

Absorbing this philosophy, members of the Japanese New Left headed off into the hills for intense sessions of self-criticism. Literally, they holed up in a mountain lodge to search and root out power and oppression among themselves. If oppression didn't occur on only large scales, but also through micropowers—such as small patterns of thought, attitudes, and stances that conveyed power and thus worked against equality—these powers must be removed from the group. Impure thoughts based on power and oppression must be expunged.

Soon these sessions sniffed out a young radical named Meiko Toyama. Toyama had the misfortune of being beautiful and attractive to the young men. For this she was turned upon; her sexual attractiveness upset the equality of the group. Proceedings spiraled into a witch hunt. The session's search for oppression, power, and radical purity turned violent, as victims began to be beaten in an attempt to force them into admitting non-pure thoughts of power and oppression. One male member was killed for asking for a tissue while in his sleeping bag, an act perceived as a kind of microaggression with dangerous sexual undertones. By the end of the self-criticism session, twelve people were dead. Fleeing members alerted the police, who laid siege to the lodge.

This rebellion was extreme and violent. It was also atypical of Japanese culture, which has an innate aversion to extreme and antisocial behavior. Yet the fact that such a reaction against cultural change emerged in Japan illuminates its lure both as a logical outcome of Kojève's thought, and as a response to the pressures of cultural change and globalization.

Politics concern power—who should have it, what should be done with it. But it also concerns human flourishing—what should be *done* with power, what is its goal, whom should it benefit. How can power liberate us from suffering? The debates on these kinds of questions are endless, and they are heating up in the West—burning hot, even, threatening to spark into an inferno. As political discourse heats up in our day, it is essential that we explore how our search for a sense of place, our drive for a borderless utopia, is driven by the further reaches of political thought.

In the following sections, I critique the foundations of two radical ideologies—the activist left and the alt-right. The goal is not to show one as more favorable than the other, but to reveal the assumptions under both, that we might be able to discern their errors, rather than fall into them.

THE ILLUSIONARY TRIUMPH OF THE NEW LEFT

The intellectual forebears of the New Left lived justified in the knowledge that they were in the minority, always on the margins culturally. In such marginality, those inspired by the thought of the New Left found it easy to commit to the doctrine of transgression. From radical university courses, extreme art shows, or punk rock gigs—at risk of being shut down by authorities, censors, and those moralizing forces in power—these rebellions accorded with the belief that evil resides in the expansive edifices of power. They were inherently against the establishment.

Now, however, leftist ideology *is* the establishment. It has become dominant in the humanities departments of almost every Western university. It is the editorial stance of major news and media sources. It even acts as a kind of moral advisor to large corporations and sporting bodies. So when the values of the New Left are orthodoxy in academia, uniform in media, delivered via family situation comedies, and propagated by the most mainstream and anodyne of teen pop stars, a problem arises: how do you hold to a worldview that decries oppression from elites, authority, and power when you *are* the elite with power?

This shift from insurgency to authoritarianism creates an existential crisis for this New Left impulse, which historically prides itself on its tolerance, open-mindedness, and the embrace of diversity. Herbert Marcuse, headmaster of the New Left, provides a bit of an "out" here with his concept of intolerant tolerance, that everything is tolerated but intolerance. According to Alasdair MacIntyre, Marcuse believed that

> human nature is indefinitely malleable. The human nature of those who inhabit advanced industrial societies has been molded so that their very wants, needs, and aspirations have become conformist— except for a minority. . . . The majority cannot voice their true needs, for they cannot perceive or feel them. The minority must therefore voice their needs for these, and this active minority must rescue the necessarily passive majority.[2]

In this feat of imagination, Marcuse offers a way for the cultural left, sworn enemies of power, authority, and conformity, to guiltlessly take the levers of power and authority with an agenda of conformity. Their ascent to power is reframed as a messianic crusade of cultural liberation, in which those who truly see the world for what it is can lead the bigoted masses into cultural enlightenment. They assume they're justified in enforcing tolerance, because who would ever defend intolerance? Semantically, tolerance is a peacemaker. "I am he as you are he as you are me and we are all together."

Marcuse predicted that such social leadership by a culturally left minority would tear down capitalist democracies from the inside. The chief way in which he envisioned this occurring was through sexual liberation. Marcuse imagined that once the West threw off its traditional Christian sexual morality, "the unpurified, unrationalized release of sexual relationships would be the strongest release of enjoyment as such and the total devaluation of labor for its own sake."[3] With sex liberated from social and moral restraints, people would never leave the bedroom, and the whole capitalist, liberal order would collapse. Central to the agenda of the New Left was the freeing of sexuality from any kind of restraint. Thus sexuality would be at the center of the New Left's culture war.

Whereas Kojève believed that an end-of-history society, in which the basic human need to be recognized as equals, was accomplished in Western liberal democracies through voting and basic rights, his New Left followers viewed liberal democracies as inherently flawed, discriminatory, and oppressive. Liberal democracies can't neutralize micropowers throughout culture and human interaction. Doctrines like free speech, freedom of religion, and free markets may be available to everyone, but they are more forceful in the hands of the powerful than the weak, and so they only perpetuate oppression. According to the New Left, liberal democracy creates freedom but does not go far enough to root out the micropowers behind all authority, language, and power. The powerful can dish out identities to those below them at will, and any such external determination of identity is an act of oppression.

As the decades passed, as the thought of the New Left developed, the range of micropowers grew. They were to be found even in the most mundane places. For example, among many of today's proponents of New Left thought, to inquire if someone has any Bangladeshi heritage, or to assume that the person you are speaking to is a particular gender, is a barefaced act of aggressive power in which "the other" is marginalized. Taking cues from the field of post-traumatic stress disorders, many colleges across the West have begun to institute "trigger warnings" on spaces or educational material that may engender negative feelings, such as the novel *The Great Gatsby*,[4] or as in Edinburgh University, where a member of the student council was removed because she had raised her hand in disagreement during a discussion, behavior that was seen as potentially "triggering."[5]

This impulse can be seen in the way that people arrange themselves in neighborhoods according to worldview or, in an extreme form, the "safe spaces" created at many universities. Individuals can easily find refuge from "micropowers of oppression" and those who will not affirm their self-determined identity. The great tragedy is that it presents those who are part of minorities, who suffer discrimination, with a hopeless view of the world, in which the challenges they face are multiplied and beleaguered on every side. It reinforces fear, because everyone is a threat. These responses lead the New Left to create its own kind of bordered safe-spaces, in which a barrier offers protections against the "flesh." And as we have discovered, once you have created a border and a place, you need to police that space, purifying it from evil and the flesh—from the "other." *The quest for absolute equality, ironically, undermines diversity.*

Westerners affirm that they value equality, diversity, and freedom, but we don't realize that these things do not necessarily act in concert. Equality of opportunity is different than equality of outcome. Communism drove toward equality of outcome, and in the process eliminated freedom. Francis Fukuyama warned that the drive for equality would become toxic once it crossed certain lines. He held that nature and fortune undermine total equality, and that a society that "seeks to eliminate every manifestation of unequal recognition . . . will quickly run into limits imposed by nature itself."

We now are back to the unfortunate Meiko Toyama, turned upon by her radical leftist comrades during their deadly self-criticism session because the beauty she was born with was seen as counter to absolute equality.[6] It is as Fukuyama warned, that the fanatical desire for equal recognition could lead to a situation where activists or those in power "try to outlaw differences between the ugly and beautiful, or pretend that a person with no legs is not just the spiritual but the physical equal of someone whole in body, [and that eventually the argument will] become self-refuting, just as communism was."[7] Here the implicit and spiritual roots of this drive for absolute equality are now being unearthed. It wishes for an equality and recognition that is beyond nature, that is supernatural.

Kojève saw the drive for equality as a Christian impulse that delayed real equality and recognition until the future fullness of heaven. Kojève, like much of modern thought, believed that we should move beyond the transcendent truths of Christianity, accepting our limitations and weaknesses as mortal human beings. The New Left drives for absolute equality, for a heavenly utopia free of oppression and evil, yet it struggles and strains to realize it in the face of the persistence of evil and the unequal contours of our world. Like all great religions try to flee the flesh via human strength, it takes on a poisonous, puritanical religious tone.

Contemporary forms of New Left thought, such as the highly fashionable area of study known as intersectionality, which sees an array of oppressions such as sexism, racism, ableism, homophobia, transphobia, and nationalism overlapping and working in concert in a vast structure of discrimination, paint an even darker picture of culture than Marcuse and Foucault (ironically mirroring the kinds of conspiracy theories found on the extremes of the right). In this vision reconciliation is impossible. It creates so many enemies in the name of self-protection that it becomes divisive and isolating. Oppression is so pervasive that one cannot escape, its infection of culture so profound as to be incurable. Marcuse's and Foucault's attempts to flee boundaries and definition, to embrace the taboo, reaches its limits of this logic, and falls back into the elemental forces.

This New Leftist impulse recognizes that forces hover behind the seats of power, yet its theories are impotent at delivering redemption. Like all human-based salvific endeavors of social engineering, it becomes fruitless religiosity. It attempts to point out the evils and faults of culture, yet pulls back from describing what a positive future may look like.[8] A demented holiness pervades, an ostentatious moralism like what Jesus warned the Pharisees against. The religious leaders of the left set up their inner courts, where only those circumcised of moral absolutism may enter. If anyone decries sexual expression or reproductive rights, or claims absolute truth, he is a Samaritan, unclean and unwelcome in the courts of the holy.

As I alluded to earlier, this newly ascendant left, keenly sniffing a victory in the culture wars, has moved from being the advocates of a new moral order to its guardians. When you are advocating for a new moral order, your tactics are insurgent. However, when you are self-imagined guardians of a moral order, your tactics must be authoritarian. No longer an insurgent, you worry about insurgent forces, past attitudes that may resurface from the dustbin of history. Like all fundamentalisms, which see the power of evil everywhere, shame, guilt and marginalization become the weapons with which to defend your moral order.

The New Left moral order increasingly begins to stiffen with a rigid and puritanical narrowness, becomes the establishment, trying to enforce its moral code from the commanding cultural heights. The great irony is that the New Left's position is actually tolerated because of power structures built on prestige and power, such as universities, government, and media. What is more, its inherent contradictions, to which it is insulated because of its rejection of dissenting views as oppressive, gives birth to a right-wing reaction.

THE RISE OF THE ALTERNATIVE RIGHT

As the left has increasingly traveled left, a new kind of right has emerged to fight back. The right, once viewed as conservative and regressive, now made taboo, is reanimated and reimagined with a transgressive, cool sheen.[9] The hip energy shifts from the cultural left to the further extremes of the right. Mimicking the activists' tactics of guilt, shame, and marginalization, mockery and trolling become legitimized in the mind of those who resist what they see as the new authoritarian left. The movement is an extremely loose and divergent movement, which arose online in reaction to the online activism of the New Left. Its genesis really began in online culture wars such as Gamergate, a battle over sexism in online computer gaming,[10] and in similar controversies in science fiction,[11] as well as on several well-known Internet hacking message boards.[12] This initial reaction began with "trolling," the baiting of hard-left figures over issues of political correctness, through Internet memes and pranks. Some elements of the movement, as it developed in reaction to the identity politics of the hard left, began to mirror a form of its own identity politics in response that in some places was nationalist, pro-male, and pro-white.

Alongside this development, in recent years, a kind of right wing reaction against globalization has grown in popularity. Institutions that are seen to be aligned with globalist philosophies such as the European Union, or the United States, are viewed negatively by the populist right, which, unlike the traditional right, favors trade barriers to protect local workers and industry from the effects of globalization. The populist right practices a kind of social conservatism. However, it is less about issues of family, gender, and sexuality and more centered on protecting native cultures from the influence of globalization, in particular large-scale immigration and political correctness.

While this new left and right snipe at each other, while those in the mainstream attempt to categorize these movements, understand them, and place them in the ill-fitting categories of the past, their influence upon culture is profound. Yet in reality the actual proponents of the alt-right, or the new intersectional left, are few. How can such marginal and extreme groups wield such influence, influencing the institutions of education, media, and politics?

One answer can be found in the New Left's attempts to undermine authority through casting doubt on all truth claims, a belief that became standard in universities across the West over the last several decades. Now we are seeing the price of that ideology. Current anxieties about "fake news," contested media narratives, and foreign government disinformation campaigns, all thrive in an environment in which authority and experts have been rejected in favor of an opinionocracy, where you decided what you wish to believe, and media silos exist in which any worldview can flourish. President Trump advisor Kellyanne Conway's use of the term "alternative facts" takes a relativist ideology of the flexibility of truth from the university humanities department right into the heart of government, creating a world where even facts are different depending on your political stripe, which Twitter silo you live within, or how you feel about them.

The myth that the Internet could give birth to a digital utopia, sealed with a cyber border from the dysfunctions, disputes, and dominations of the real world, has now been destroyed. Web 2.0, that is the major social networks, video platforms such as YouTube, and blogs, have accelerated the blurring of the lines between truth and fiction. As Andrew Keen writes, "This undermining of truth is threatening the quality of civil public discourse, encouraging plagiarism and intellectual property theft, and stifling creativity . . . the line between fact and fiction becomes blurred. Instead of more community, knowledge, or culture, all that Web 2.0 really delivers is more dubious content."[13]

The extremes of left and right always rise together, and so it is with the alt-right and hard left. Like two alligators fighting to the death in a swamp, their combat spurs each other on to greater extremes. The Internet has created a forum in which this battle flows into popular culture, and is highlighted in our mainstream and social media. During the 1930s, the new far right copied the tactics of the far left, like street fighting, protests, and targeting individuals and businesses. Now the same patterns repeat, but online.

The New Left, sensing triumph in the culture wars, believing the arc of history on their side, believing the myth each generation to be more progressive than the next, now faces their worst nightmare. An insurgent, millennial-driven, post-traditional, post-modern, post-Christian, Internet-driven reactionary movement, which copies their tactics, using irony, mockery, and humor to disguise a far-right political platform. As the *New York Times* columnist Ross Douthat recently noted, in the New Left and alt-right we are beginning to see first signs of truly post-Christian politics,[14] a world without forgiveness, which seeks not compromise but the utter humiliation of one's cultural and political enemies. A political discourse, shaped by the unrestrained ego, and the concept of the leader who sacrifices for the people, but instead enriches oneself, while revenge-tweeting.

The ferocity of this battle threatens to overrun mainstream politics, adding to the sense of cultural emergency, and contributing to the atmosphere of outrage and anxiety. The litany of hurts and wounds of each side leads the political battle into more ferocious territory. Compromise and meeting in the middle descends into total political and cultural war, facilitated over digital networks to which we are constantly connected. Creating a feverish mood, and an incendiary culture.

In the next chapter, I'll address where this growing tension may lead the West. The social structures and movements bouncing this way and that in our world have spiritual forces behind them and, thus, require spiritual solutions.

CHAPTER 8

CULTURAL DIFFUSION

With culture overrun by anxiety and an increasingly confusing culture war between an activist left and a reactive
right, the question for many Christians is: *Will such upheaval
draw those in the West back to faith?* This question is explored in
Michel Houellebecq's novel *Submission*. Set in Paris in the year
2020, it explores the descent of secular French citizens into
decadence.

In the book, France is in the grip of a presidential election,
in which the real-life far-right leader Marine Le Pen is about
to seize power. In order to prevent this move to the right, the
mainstream parties form an alliance with a Muslim party, paving
the way for France to reject secularism and return to being a
religious nation, albeit Islamic rather than Christian. Inci-
dentally, the novel was released on the same day that Islamic
militants massacred the editorial staff of the magazine *Charlie
Hebdo*. However in *Submission,* the jihadists are absent, and in
their place are urbane and reasonable Islamic politicians and in-
fluencers. The Islamic characters in the novel are decent and fair.

The protagonist of the book, François, a literary professor

approaching middle age, is symbolic of the cultural decadence of the secular West. With the meaning of literature deconstructed, and thus no longer offering solace, François drifts in a sea of options. His life is a study of living in a non-place. Purchases online, takeaway dinners delivered to his door, Internet pornography, and a steady stream of students willing to offer him sex minus commitment, an illustration of how consumerism has replaced religion as the guiding social force. François has endless freedoms, the ability to satiate his animal desires with the click of his mouse, yet he is alone and directionless. With the death of his parents, and his own personal aging, he reaches an existential crisis brought on by cultural exhaustion, fainting in the face of the drudgery of constant pleasure, distraction, and stimulation. He discovers that a non-place is no place to live.

Unlike his literary hero and subject of study, the nineteenth-century author Joris-Karl Huysmans, who after a life of the decadent pursuit of pleasure returned to the church, Christ is unattractive to François. Instead, like the future France of Houellebecq's imagination, François halfheartedly drifts toward Islam. It is more a collapse than a conversion. The exhaustion of freedom, the cost of France's secular religion of liberty is passivity, isolation, boredom, and lostness. In the place of liberty and freedom, the root of the word *Islam*—submission. The certainty of submission to divine will. Houellebecq seems to be wagering that the once thought-of inevitable march of secularism could be undone by the cultural exhaustion that unlimited freedom brings. The boredom that arises at the end of history.

Houellebecq's Franco-Islamic state in the harsh light of day seems unlikely. Nor do I think that he believes it is inevitable or even possible. Rather, it is a satirical dig at an exhausted West, in particular a French political and cultural left, so blindly opposed to the boundaries, authorities, and traditionalism of the European conservative right, that they would willingly submit to rule by the even more boundary-setting, authoritarian, and non-Western traditionalism embodied in Islam.

What do we make of our exhausted West? It is pining for something, certainly. Even the most secular among us would agree that the world is a mess. But still, bound by the flesh, the West is searching for freedom where it will not find it. In this chapter I explore how the West has turned to decadence and comfortability, only to discover it has led to the extreme discomfort of cultural diffusion. The West has run itself dizzy, and there is only one way to find equilibrium.

DECADENCE VERSUS THE END OF HISTORY

Long ago, a great number of thinkers worried that complete freedom, equality, and decadence would lead to decay, collapse, and even tyranny. For example, Plato warned of an excess of equality in which parents no longer taught and disciplined. Parents who act like children themselves, the old would try and impress the young in a cult of youth. Teachers would fear offending those in their care and thus fawn over their students. Competition and chaos would mark family and social life. Citizens would develop a commitment phobia. The desires of necessity give way to the desires of luxury, as some fall into decadent hedonism. Those who pursue a dissolute life become envious of those who delay gratification, work hard, and thus find wealth. Society becomes divided, anxiety takes hold, and politics become full of false promises and slander. The people turn to strong men to advocate for them against the other side. One strong man emerges dominant, however. Corrupted by the pursuit of desires, he becomes despotic and the people lose their freedom.[1]

The great medieval Arabic scholar Ibn Khaldun observed a four-generational pattern that corrupted civilizations. A first generation struggles from adversity and deprivation to create stability and wealth. The second generation, enjoying the benefits of the newly created wealth and security, is closely mentored by the previous generation in the traditions and wisdoms that enabled this wealth. The third generation, disconnected from the influence of the first generation, must follow the precepts of success and security as a blind tradition, and thus becomes a less efficient mentor. The fourth generation, taking their wealth and stability as a naturally occurring state of affairs, seeing it as a privilege and entitlement, is now distanced from their civilization's founding principles and sacrifices. Thus they come to despise, doubt, and eventually reject the traditions that secured their culture's wealth and security, and are plunged back into deprivation and adversity as they are overrun by hungrier and more disciplined competitors.[2]

Houellebecq's fellow Frenchman Alexis de Tocqueville, observing favorably the democratic freedom and equality in the nineteenth-century United States, cautioned that tyranny could emerge from democracy in the future. To ensure that this would not happen, he saw bulwarks against decadence and tyranny in the morality of religion. He viewed volunteer-driven, local, mediating religious and civic institutions as fortifications against the tyranny of a despot, the precise kinds of institutions that have been hollowed out in recent decades. Tocqueville felt most uneasy about a society in which individualism existed alongside a powerful government, which wished to benignly and gently control an increasing level of citizens' lives, and in the process would "degrade men without tormenting them"[3]—a situation that looks worryingly like our current context.

CULTURAL DIFFUSION

If decadence gives way to entitlement and severe individualism, then cultural diffusion naturally follows. That is, shared cultural platforms break. Take, for example, the liberalizing, modernistic dynamic that powers globalization. It is resisted by both the left and the right, but in different ways. Conservatives celebrate the freeing of markets and the internationalizing of trade that globalization brings, but bemoans the way it has eaten away at morals and values. Those on the left applaud the cultural liberalization that globalization brings, but they bemoan the way markets spread economic inequality. So the right and the left, deciding who's responsible for the decaying of culture, point to each other.

Societal diffusion, which fragments meanings and creates a diminishing consensus, means it becomes harder to tell consistent stories about our culture. Our culture grows both in scale and incomprehension. Diffusion means the spread of elements; it is the opposite of concentration. The elements of culture spread widely without boundaries, mixing up with everything else. This wide dispersal means culture becomes more fragile.

This also changes who has perceived power. Moises Naim reports that "for many decades, even centuries, barriers to power sheltered massive armies, corporations, governments, parties, and social and cultural institutions. Now those barriers are crumbling, eroding, leaking, or being rendered otherwise irrelevant."[4] Power is now spread across an ever-expanding base of players. The large-scale institutions still have power but are constrained in how they use it. Microplayers have greater ability to disrupt and influence. The result is a new kind of situation in which all feel beleaguered, all are trolled, and all sides believe that someone else is in power.

A more connected world, and becoming more rapidly connected each day, becomes what William H. Davidow calls *overconnected*. This is "what happens to a system when connectivity increases dramatically both inside and outside of it, and parts if not the whole system are unable to adjust."[5] Connectivity increases our opportunities but also the threats we face. The erasure of boundaries opens the world up to us, but also endangers us, creating something more complicated than decay. Cultural reactions, declines, and revivals occur simultaneously—like an explosion in a chemistry lab, where solutions mix rapidly together. New elements are formed. The old institutions and traditions are all there, but they are weakened. The power now rests with the diffusers, such as Apple and Google, which are able to spread information far and wide, which attempt to control and navigate the new complexity but also add to it.

CAPTURE THE CULTURE? WHAT CULTURE?

For those wishing to command a culture, globalization presents insurmountable odds. Small, committed elites determined to change the agenda of culture march into treacherous and foggy terrain, often becoming lost, unable to determine a read on the actual lay of the land. Once a sector of culture is taken hold of, whether by conservatives or progressives, that stronghold is almost impossible to defend, for the disruptive, anti-authoritarian nature of our diffused world turns upon power. This is true even when power is held by those who are anti-power and anti-authoritarian, such as the New Left. As Levin writes:

> If cultural liberals imagine that they are now in decisive command of our mainstream culture and its institutions, they will be making the same mistake some cultural conservatives made in recent decades—ignoring the fact of our diffusing society and undermining their own capacity to appeal to a broad public outside their narrow circle of the converted . . . the social left is a minority, too, and it is a minority aspiring to dominate our institutions at a time when those institutions are particularly weak and diffuse.[6]

In other words, it doesn't matter how loud your microphone is; you cannot command who isn't listening. People don't like being preached at. The left learned this in the 2016 US presidential election.

The right faces a similar challenge. Its hope rests in the fact that what it sees as the morally bankrupt excesses of the left will result in a moral rallying and return to conservative values.

Instead we are seeing the emergence of a post-religious and post-traditional populist conservatism. However, because of the diffused nature of society, in each generation there will be rediscoveries of progressive thought. It is never vanquished, but rediscovered in multiple ways, as the diffused, unequal society creates a desire among new generations to right the wrongs. The right faces its sternest challenge not from its enemies on the left, but those on the further reaches of the right. Thus taking the culture, be it for progressive, conservative, or even religious motivations—in this moment of diffusion—becomes a quixotic quest. An attempt to herd cats.

WHAT DOES THIS MEAN FOR THE CHURCH?

The chaos will not disappear. We may wish for a return to a time of stability, and the world may for moments seem to settle and calm, but this does not accord with a biblical view of the world. Dissolution is here to stay. Scripture speaks of a chaos in the world that waits to break out at any moment. Like the sea smashing against the cliffs, fighting against restraints, this chaos threatens to flood the world.

However, to temporarily hold this chaos at bay, God has established bulwarks. The apostle Paul, describing the reality and spiritual power behind our nations, our places, our cultures and institutions, takes the term "the powers." The powers are the unseen superstructures behind human life, and, just like places, nations, institutions, they protect us from the chaos in the world that threatens to break through.

Colossians explains that the powers were created by God. "For in him all things were created: things in heaven and on earth, visible and invisible, whether thrones or powers or rulers or authorities; all things have been created through him and for him" (Col. 1:16 NIV). However, these powers fell, rebelling against God. In his letter to the Ephesians, Paul writes that the believer is now in battle with these powers. "For our battle is not against flesh and blood, but against the rulers, against the authorities, against the world powers of this darkness, against the spiritual forces of evil in the heavens" (Eph. 6:12).

For countless generations these compromised and degraded powers have attempted to play their role of keeping chaos at bay. Yet instead of being buffers against the chaos, they become barriers between people and God, realms in which humans could exercise dominion apart from God. Like faulty life-preservers, they kept some above the waters, and others they let drown. Yet what was consistent with their role is that they could not save; they could only delay the inevitable. A Savior needed to come.

And come He did. Jesus' redemptive action on the cross was a crushing defeat of the rebellious powers.

Paul's description of the defeat of the powers in Colossians is illuminating. He writes that Christ "disarmed the rulers and authorities and disgraced them publicly; He triumphed over them by Him" (Col. 2:15). These are terms and images taken directly from Roman political life. The way in which Caesars and generals would defeat foreign kings and peoples, taking their weapons, marching them in chains, through the streets of Rome, to kneel before the throne of their conqueror. The fearsome barbarian king, causing mayhem far away on the fringes of the Empire. Rumors and imagination inflating their monstrous size and power in the minds of the Roman people. However, as they were led through the streets in chains, their larger-than-life reputations would shrink. The curtain would be pulled back, and the feeble person behind the myth exposed.

The powers have been exposed in the same way. Promising a tall wall against the forces of flesh and chaos, their impotency has been revealed by Christ. The naked, humiliating truth that they cannot save—that they were frauds all along—is now on display for all to see. A disenchanting of the world has occurred; Jesus' victory on the cross has exposed the spiritual superstructure behind the myths, powers, and gods that humans looked to for solace from the chaos.

This is the good news of the gospel. Humans no longer have to be bound to these myths and powers. Those trying to scratch out Eden in the dust don't have to anymore. There is a way out of the fray. And for those who already have come to believe the gospel, and who feel displaced and dizzy in all the chaos, this truth remains a comfort. All the powers swarming around us, most of them beyond our understanding, have been disarmed. Yes, they are still active, but only in the same way a chicken is after its head is cut off.

All our human programs, our desire for home, for place. Our Babel-infused dreams of an enlightened, placeless utopia, our political programs both left and right, our individual seeking for satisfaction, all come to naught. Creation still groans. Self, blood, soil, technology, ideology, religiosity cannot save us. The only hope is found in the Savior, who would come and die. Triumphing above all the powers, the principalities, the elemental forces of the world, over you and me. The only truth, the only way, the only answer, found in the re-patterned life, that emerges from God.

PART 3

LIFE RE-PATTERNED

IN THE
SPIRIT

CHAPTER 9

THE CHURCH IN BATTLE

As the church looks ahead at the days to come, she of course cannot know exactly what to expect. Predictions are fraught with danger. The election of Donald Trump, as well as Britons voting to leave the EU, took pollsters, media, and those who make a living predicting which way the cultural winds will blow totally by surprise, so blinded they were by their own predilections and social bubble. Yesterday's marginal thought, or seemingly redundant social movement, can spring back with a vengeance.

However, Scripture can inform us at least of the contours of our future by informing us of the realities of the human heart. We have learned that the nations will always rage, wishing to cast off the restraints that God has placed upon them. Humans will always attempt to fill the desire that can only be met by God in other things. Christ's victory on the cross has defeated the powers; they have been exposed and humiliated, yet they still flail and injure. Disorder will continue, not because we are entering a particularly disordered time, but because human history inevitably will be disordered until Christ ends the age.

We struggle with this because we bought the myth that history had ended, and that we could enjoy a kind of heaven on earth existence without God.

Humbly speculating, I believe the trends sketched in this book will continue. The tensions and opportunities created by globalization will not go away. The future will be fragmented and diffused. Cultural, ideological, political, and religious programs, which attempt to communicate to and capture the "culture" or the "general public," will soon discover that such an entity does not exist. Walter Lippmann warned decades ago that it was a mistake to "conclude that the public is in some deep way a messianic force."[1] A key to unlock culture. Rather, the nations of the West have become many subcultures, which retreat, mutate, react, and hybridize. Political and cultural elites struggle and scramble to create uniting myths, establish new cultural norms, enforce freshly minted moral codes, and yet celebrate the diversity beneath them, forever confronted with the fear of incoherence and breakdown. All groups will feel embattled and fragile, seeing their opponents in control of the commanding heights of influence.

THREATS FACING THE CHURCH

The church must be vigilant moving forward, as she faces a number of threats. The threats are varied, and sometimes opposing, but they all share one origin: elemental forces. Writing to the church in Galatia, Paul notes that before Christ came, we were like children guarded by the law (Gal. 3:23), echoing language used in the ancient world to describe guardians who would ensure that youth made it to school.[2] Yet Christ had changed everything, welcoming us as co-heirs, as we have been adopted by God to be His sons and daughters. So Paul offers a warning. "In the past, when you didn't know God, you were enslaved to things that by nature are not gods. But now, since you know God, or rather have become known by God, how can you turn back to the weak and bankrupt elemental forces?" (Gal. 4:8–9). Paul's accusation, Peter Leithart points out, is that "by reverting to Torah, the Galatians have turned back to those same elementary things rather than accepting the inheritance that has now come to them."[3] Paul implored his followers not to return to slavery in any form, a very real threat to their young faith.

All around them, pagan Greco-Roman worship abounded. Between shrines at the crossroads, gods of tradesmen and guilds, foreign gods in wide array, mystery religions, and esoteric wisdoms to be explored and lost in, a religiously dense landscape presented countless opportunities for worship and homage. It was a world dedicated to purity, sacrifice, and sacred boundaries, peppered with temples and filled with worshipers. Thus Paul asks the Galatians regarding the elemental forces, "Do you want to be enslaved to them all over again? You observe special days, months, seasons, and years. I am fearful for you, that perhaps my labor for you has been wasted" (Gal. 4:9–11). Those who had known the gospel, who had bent their knee to the king who humiliated and triumphed over the powers, faced the temptation to return to them, to be enslaved again. However, with the powers humiliated, with Christ triumphant, they could not truly go back—there was nothing, truly, to go back to—instead they could only fall into the realm of heresy. *The church in Galatia, like the other seminal churches of*

*the first century, and indeed like churches in every era, could only
distort and disfigure Christianity; they could not undo it.*

As the gospel was preached, as history unfolded, Christ's
victory over the powers would spread. The elemental forces
had been fundamentally altered, and a new kingdom had
broken in, and thus the powers gradually lost their hold over
people. However, as Christianity spread, so did heresy.

The church father Tertullian is often quoted as saying that
the true gospel is always found between the twin temptations of irreligion and religion. Most heresies too fall into
these categories. Some heresies take freedom in Christ and
run madly with it, breaking well beyond the bounds of God's
creational order and revelation, sinning because Christ has set
us free (Romans 6). Others reject the freedom of the gospel for
self-sufficiency. Returning to the seeming safety and strength of
the elemental forces, they double down on religiosity and programs that earn salvation through human endeavor. One says,
"I may do anything," the other, "I must do everything," but a
Christian says, "Christ has done what I can't do, so I am free to
do it" (see Rom. 8:1–8).

It is not a coincidence that many of our Western church
models were formed and shaped in the age of optimism that
followed the fall of the Berlin Wall. Individuals—raised, edu-
cated, and formed by this unusual time—found their expectations conflicting with reality. Unprepared for discomfort, they
developed life strategies that assumed the age of optimism was
normative. Churches can fall into the same trap, and many individuals can fall into melancholy and anxiety when they discover
that the age of optimism was not normative.

Melancholic, anxious, and pining for the warmer days of the past, churches, Christian organizations, and believers can find themselves retreating from their God-given mandate, forgetting their prime place in Christ's mission to win the world. Instead of providing a shining alternative light to the anxiety and despair of the surrounding culture, we can simply be a mirror reflecting its worries. For when we look at the world through a biblical lens, we see God's relentless love for humanity, His victory over sin and the powers, His desire to move beyond borders, and His gospel spreading to the ends of the earth.

The Western church, blessed with incredible resources, astounding knowledge, and know-how can find itself paralyzed by anxiety. Michael Goheen notes that the church in the West's ability to respond to its high call can be hamstrung by "a low spiritual state of the church, a lukewarm love for Christ, a sickly worldliness, and a lack of vital prayer." Goheen's diagnosis of why this is so accords with the contours of the age of optimism: "self-satisfaction that comes from comfort, compromise with capitalism, and accommodation to the consumeristic spirit of our age."[4] Now, however, that self-satisfaction, exhausted by possibility, and worried by the upheaval in the world, recoils from the cost of God's mandate, retreating into comfort yet falling into the flesh.

As these factors trend into the future, more churches will inevitably twist and turn in response. In such an environment the church will continue being tempted to take three main shapes. Some churches will reshape themselves as kinds of Christian non-places, detached from history, relationships, and given identity. They will be chaplains of self-realization, helping individuals live comfortably in the non-place of globalization—essentially giving a Christian sheen to the utopia of globalization. They'll deliver tips and life hacks for living life to the fullest, a new kind of prosperity gospel for the no-places of globalization. "Repent" will nearly disappear from their vernacular. The battle against the flesh and sin will be replaced with a program to inflate self-esteem.

Other churches, attuned to the dislocation and meaningless-ness created by the non-place of globalization, will fiercely create nationalist, social, and racial boundaries, presenting meanings that emerge not from Christ and the kingdom, but place, nation, myth, and the flesh. In one sense, cultural Christianity is dying across the West; people are recognizing where church and state rub up against each other. In another sense, though, a new kind of cultural Christianity is emerging, sometimes taking old terms such as "evangelical" or "born-again Christian" and reinterpreting them to land miles from their original meaning. Less concerned with sexual morality, churchgoing, and the discipline of discipleship, it rather attempts to respond to the effects of globalization by pushing back minority cultures—a dangerous dance with blood, soil, and flag. It loses itself in conspiracy theories and speculative, politicized reimaginings of Armageddon. This moves into even more dangerous territory in the alt-right. Journalist Michael Knowles writes, "The Alt-Right loves Christendom but rejects Christianity." They see Christendom as the forge of the West, but actual Christianity as something that needs to be moved beyond. Knowles quotes alt-right thinker Stephen McNallen describing himself, like many alt-right figures do, as a pagan who rejects Christianity because it "lacks any roots in blood or soil."[5]

A third group of churches, recoiling both from the implicit prosperity gospel of the churches that create Christian non-places, and disturbed by the falling back into cultural Christianity and the blurring of nationalism and the way of Jesus, will link arms with the New Left. Finding solace and succor in its agenda of equality and justice, and sensing the biblical prophetic parallels, it blindly misses its contradictions. Its motor isn't fueled by the Spirit, but the flesh. Ironically, it will flee what it sees as the reactive conservatism and hyper-religiosity of cultural Christianity only to be entrapped by the reactive progressivism and hyper-religiosity of the extremes of the left.

THE CHURCH'S RESPONSE

If these three responses won't do, then what is the better alternative? The answer is to fight the good fight. We the church, we as individual believers, have bought the end-of-history myth that comfort and peace are normative. A simple reading of the Bible tells us this is not the case, has not been the case since Eden, and will never be the case until the Lord returns. Kojève, who introduced the end-of-history concept, was wrong about a lot, but he got one thing right: humans are born for a fight. If war and struggle are absent, we will hunt for something to fight about. We seek out struggle, we create conflict. It's in our blood.

In *Tribe,* war correspondent Sebastian Junger explores why so many returning soldiers struggle upon returning home. Junger, who himself suffers from post-traumatic stress disorder incurred on the battlefield, notes that it is not just the horror of war, but the banality of civilian life in the West, which causes soldiers much distress. Conflict is terrible, but it reduces life down to life-and-death essentials. Junger notes that the camaraderie of battle for many veterans cannot be replaced by the low-level relationality of contemporary life. Their military service gave them a deeper kind of tribal connection, one built around difficulty, challenge, battle, and suffering.

Civilians can also share this tribal connection. Junger recalls covering the siege of Sarajevo during the fall of Yugoslavia, and hearing residents struggle with the fact that despite all the suffering they experienced, they felt a strange sense of sentimentality about the siege. The same happened in the Battle of Britain, in which those who lived through the bombing looked back fondly at the blitz for how it drew them together.[6] Junger notes the social effects that followed the attacks of September 11. Suicide and depression rates dropped, use of pharmacological drugs declined, and those suffering from the effects of post-traumatic stress disorder reported an improvement in their symptoms. Church attendance even increased. New York, mocked and maligned for the coldness of its radical individualism, saw a flowering of community mindedness.

We see a similar effect in a phenomenon known as the "immigrant paradox."[7] For some time, health professionals assumed that some of the most unhealthy people in the West would be those who had migrated from the developing world. Facing challenges such as integration, racism, and difficulties in finding work, and coming from nations with lower standards of health care, one might expect immigrants to be unhealthier and suffer greater mental health challenges. But over time the opposite proved true. Immigrants turned out to be healthier than those native born. The West, which offered better access to nutritional food and advanced health care, was superior environmentally to the developing world, and thus improved the health of migrants. In fact, it was when migrants became more integrated, learned second languages, and followed fewer of their own rituals, patterns, and behaviors, and instead adopted more Western customs, that their health deteriorated to the level of the native born.

The root of these assumptions is that hardship inhibits health. Surely obstacles of language, unemployment, and even prejudice would take a toll on migrants mentally and physically. Interestingly, though, Westerners who did not face hardship, opposition, and persecution were more depressed and unhealthy. Newly arrived immigrants could live on the same soil, access the same institutions, breathe the same air, drive the same roads, and walk the same paths, and arrive at a very different standard of physical health and mental well-being than those born in that environment. The difference is contemporary Western culture—not just the ideas and ideologies, but the way in which we are formed and shaped by those ideologies. Our unhindered comfort not only makes us spiritually sick but mentally and physically weak. We are like astronauts coming back from space, muscles atrophied after months of zero gravity. Our lack of hardship weakens our resilience.

We are born for struggle, created for a cause, formed for a great battle. We as individuals find meaning in struggle. And the church is God's army. However, in the West she has been away from battle far too long. Not only has she forgotten how to fight, but she's forgotten that she's in battle. What is more, she's come to expect peace. Resistance is foreign to her. "What battle?" she says. The armor of God is gathering dust in the corner.

Of course, if we are not careful, such talk of battle and struggle can lead us back into the dangerous ground of the elemental forces, to a religion of earthly violence, force, and oppression. We may respond to an increasingly forceful, material, striving culture by seeking to carve out the kingdom of God through human force. That's not what's in mind here, though. In the words of Jacques Ellul, the church is called to "true *spiritual* violence, based on earnest faith: faith in the possibility of a miracle, in the Lordship of Jesus Christ, and in the coming of the kingdom through God's action"[8] (emphasis mine). We wage peace, not war, in the power of Christ and His loving Spirit. We are not set against human flesh and blood, as Paul warns us in Ephesians, but against the powers and principalities—the attitudes and mindsets that oppose God, which attempt autonomy apart from God. We attack them not with flaming angry tweets, lawsuits, Kalashnikov assault rifles, or predator drones, but with the Word of God. The sharing and preaching of the gospel, the loving witness of the people of God. Such things are spiritually violent, only because they are repugnant to the forces of flesh that rebel against God, which flee from His goodness. Therefore the fruit of the Spirit, when hurled against the flesh, turn into grenades in God's great last battle to redeem the world. When the Word of God pierces someone, it saves them.

This is the great battle of our time—not merely of our current historical moment, but of the great epoch that is the end times, the period between Christ's death and resurrection and His promised return. In this period, we are called to a battle.

We will not find comfort in this battle, but we will find joy and meaning, for, in the words of Peter Leithart, "The Spirit is at war with flesh, outside and within the church, and it is the duty of the church's members and leaders to stay in the ranks of the Spirit as he carries out that warfare and not abandon the Spirit to join forces with the flesh." His encouragement continues, pointing us toward the church as the place in which the fight against the flesh is to be conducted:

> After the resurrection, because of the resurrection, the new physics of social and political life that began to take form in Jesus' ministry persisted among his disciples, a community that combines all nations to call all the nations to die to flesh and join the ranks of the Spirit. This twofold movement of death-and-resurrection, of condemnation and vindication, is God's act of justification through the faith of Jesus Christ. It is God's act that establishes a just human society on earth . . . Now at last the life of Spirit in flesh is a reality among humankind.[9]

I doubt we are at the end of history as either Kojève or Fukuyama predicted. However, I believe both were right, at least in how what we imagined as the end of history, in which humans were to be satisfied by peace and consumer plenty, may fail humans. Kojève saw a tragedy in the arrival of such a world. And so must we, for such an arrival falls well short of the coming kingdom, which Christ will usher in fully. *Thus our meaning is to be found in the battle between flesh and the Spirit.* We will continue exploring this in the coming chapters.

CHAPTER 10

LIFE IN THE SPIRIT

In John's Gospel, we find Jesus exemplifying the new kind of life in the Spirit that will mark the coming church. Pausing at a Samaritan well, Jesus requests a drink of water from a woman. A seemingly mundane and inconsequential act, but one that crosses two major taboos. For a man to engage a woman, who was not his kin, in conversation was a major taboo. Not just any woman, but a Samaritan woman. A people group that represented another boundary to the Jewish nation. Samaritans posed a danger, for they were kinds of half-Jews, hybrids. To faithful Jews, they were an impure blending of true faith with idolatry and polytheism. With His simple request for a drink of water, Jesus had sliced through two heavily fortified social barriers, one based on race and religion, the other on gender.

Shocked by His social impropriety, the woman informs Jesus of the social barriers He is leaping over, stating indignantly what may mask a level of intrigue, "How is it that You, a Jew, ask for a drink from me, a Samaritan woman?" (John 4:9). Jesus refuses to entertain a discussion on such divisions, turning the conversation by insisting that the woman is missing the point. The Samaritan woman is unaware of who is before her. Unaware that Jesus can provide living water. Again the woman operates on the level of the elemental forces, bringing the conversation back to what divides Jews and Samaritans, attempting to pridefully assert that the well that Jesus is drinking from, Jacob's well, belongs to her people, not His. Jesus again speaks of living water. A water that gives eternal life. Finally her thought ascends from the concreteness of land, place, and people, and grasps the good news Jesus brings.

After cutting through major social taboos and cultural borders, Jesus erects a moral barrier, revealing that the woman has had more than just one husband, many, and that the man she is currently with is not her husband. Amazed at Jesus' ability to see into the deepest parts of her soul, the woman at this point can still pull back. Jesus is offering a different kind of life, one flowing with living water, born of the Spirit. He is offering her a way into the now present life of God. She can buck, rebel, still choose the way of the flesh, pull back from the border that requires we leave behind our autonomy, pride, and sin. One last time the woman attempts to wrest the conversation back to the elemental forces, the childish simplicity of place and pride. She notes His spiritual insight, accepting that He must be a prophet, yet wishes to quibble over the differing opinions of where Jews and Samaritans believe worship should occur. Jesus lovingly and transcendently replies,

> "Believe Me, woman, an hour is coming when you will worship the Father neither on this mountain nor in Jerusalem. You Samaritans worship what you do not know. We worship what we do know, because salvation

is from the Jews. But an hour is coming, and is now here, when the true worshipers will worship the Father in spirit and truth. Yes, the Father wants such people to worship Him. God is spirit, and those who worship Him must worship in spirit and truth." (John 4:21–24)

Jesus' words point to a new phase in human history, a deep shift at the core of the world, a new way of being human. Humans no longer needed to shelter behind their defensive structures, shuddering in fear of the flesh. Nor would they need to fear sabotage from within their defensive structures as their flesh overran them. Spirit and truth now superseded place.

The elemental building blocks of the cosmos changed a short time later at Jesus' crucifixion. It was, however, a change that had occurred under cover of dark. The nocturnal signs were there, as graves belched up the dead, the ground shook, and the sun was eclipsed. However, the temple stood strong, so did the geomancy of the Roman state, its statues, columns, forts, temples, and palaces.

SPIRIT VERSUS CONCRETE

As the moon cleared the sun, and its rays again illuminated the world, nothing seemed to have changed. One needed new eyes to see the transformation. The tell was the curtain in the temple. The veil protecting humans from the purity of God, and God from the impurity of human flesh, ripped from top to bottom. Not a work of human hands, not an extension of the project of Babel, the drive of humans to cross the divide between human and God. This was God coming close, crossing the chasm carved out by human hands, the high point of His great love for humankind. Jesus had redeemed the flesh by living in the flesh in unbroken communion with the Father, falling not into sin, choosing faith instead of fear, obedience instead of rebellion.

Having seen the empty tomb, having received the risen Christ as a visitor in their midst, the disciples and followers of Jesus, filled with wonder, fear, and questions, began to coagulate into something new. Still, at this stage, Charles Williams reminds us they remained "a small secret group in Jerusalem. They supposed themselves to be waiting for the new manifestation which had been promised, in order that they might take up the work which their Lord had left them."[1] The time for secrets, however, was over; the powers had been defeated, the sinfulness of flesh routed by the cross.

The new manifestation came suddenly. "At a particular moment, and by no means secretly, the heavenly Secrets opened upon them, and there was communicated to that group of Jews, in a rush of wind and a dazzle of tongued flames, the secret of the Paraclete in the Church."[2] Williams uses here the Greek term for the Spirit, a helper, a counselor, a guide, reminding us of His beautiful strangeness.

The Spirit fell upon the disciples as they were meeting in a room. Rooms by their nature are closed off, sealed off from nature and the world through their walls; entry is gained through crossing hearths, doors, and curtains, barriers with which to seal the purity of the room. The Spirit falls, just as He had fallen upon Jesus at the beginning of His ministry as He waded into the Jordan River, the barrier Israel crossed to enter into the

Promised Land. The disciples, joyful and filled with fire and Spirit, almost emerge from the dark, enclosed space of their room, the barrier that had sealed off the secret of the resurrection from the world, tumbling into the street. They babble in foreign tongues. The scene seems so ridiculous to uninformed eyes; they incur the mockery of passersby, who presume the architect of this unusual scene is alcoholic spirits, but as they will soon discover it is the Spirit.

An early morning drunken reverie was not the form the church would take. Otherwise, it would be mistakenly dismissed as another ecstatic mystery cult, like those who worshiped the gods of wine, chaos, and pleasure. Liber, Bacchus, or Dionysius, celebrating chaos with booze, song, and dance. Rather, this was a celebration of the crossing of a barrier, a blockade, the passing into a promised land. Williams reflects, "This was but a demonstration, as it were; the real work was now to begin, and the burden of the work was accepted by the group in the city. That work was the regeneration of mankind. The word has, too often, lost its force; it should be recovered. The apostles set out to generate mankind anew."[3] Their fall into the street, their crossing of the barrier of private into public, secret into proclamation, is not driven by human will or endeavor; rather it is powered by the Spirit. The Spirit who now allows humans to draw close to God. There is no need for purified temples, spiritual veils, and atoning animal sacrifices. The church, the new community, which gathers around the Lordship of Christ, had already been glimpsed during Jesus' ministry.

A NEW BOUNDARY

The barriers of language and culture erected in defense against the fleshly tower of Babel are now crossed. Jews from across the world, who had traveled to the holy city of Jerusalem to worship and sacrifice at the temple, now find the believers speaking in the comforting familiarity of their mother tongues. History has shifted. As Williams accounts, "The Spirit took his own means to found and to spread Christendom before a single apostolic step had left Jerusalem . . . He prepared the way himself."[4] *The elemental forces, the magnetism of Jerusalem and the temple had been reversed.* The Spirit spinning outwards into the world, creating a new spiritual dynamic, which sped past borders, barriers, and blockages. The mythological power of Rome had been defeated without a sword being drawn. Its defeat not coming from a crossing of the Rubicon, but through the transgressing of an unseen boundary, the border of baptism.

"Baptism is a boundary-establishing ritual,"[5] notes Wayne A. Meeks. Crossing this barrier did not require a death, but rather a death to self, death to the agenda of the flesh, death to a willful attempt to conquer our weakness and mortality. It was not crossed with heroic power; rather it was a collapse, a giving up of all human striving, a falling into the water and the arms of Christ. In contrast to the pomp and splendor of the surrounding civil religions—the ritualized forms of worship and sacrifice. The worship of the Christians, the wine, the bread, the sung songs, the hands raised in prayer, the read Scripture, and apostolic letters in apartments, and catacombs, to external eyes, would seem paltry. However, God was forming not monuments or myths but people who lived by the Spirit. These people were being developed into a new kind of humans who did not influence via the flesh. "Baptism into Jesus Christ meant a total resocialization, in which loyalty to the Christian group was supposed to replace every other loyalty,"[6] writes James S. Jeffers. They existed as a kind of creative minority, engaged in an asymmetrical war against flesh.

One could no longer bow their knees to the myths, gods, and powers of the world for they understood that they had been defeated by the cross. This minority was forced into a strange paradox of belonging in the world, but not truly. They were, as Scripture states, in the world but not of it. The world, meaning not the physical earth but rather the social and cultural universe humans create and set against God, could no longer shelter these people, the church. They were no longer truly home in "place." They had taken a step back from the elemental forces; their allegiance was to God and the space in which His will reigns. They understood that the tilt of history pointed to the time in which that reign would cover the land and the seas and in which all knees would bow, and tongues confess.

* * * * *

Moving forward into the future, the church, in the battle with flesh, living for the Spirit, the people of God would have a creative mandate, their mere presence a rebuke to the elemental forces, an ongoing humiliation to the powers and principalities. As Arthur Glasser explains,

> What this means is that Christians in the world have a role to fill that non-Christians cannot possibly fill. They have to break the fatality that hangs over the

world through reflecting in every way the victory that Christ gained over the powers. They are to be a sign of the new covenant, a demonstration that the new order has entered the world, giving meaning, direction, and hope to history. This means that Christians dare not uncritically and automatically reflect even the best of the world's patterns of conduct, social amelioration, and service. The world's agenda and the world's methodology are not to be theirs, largely because the motivation behind their activities will shape their service differently. And the powers must be confronted with this.[7]

Glasser's comments mark an excellent spot with which to begin exploring the church's role in our current moment. With the powers humiliated and defeated, Marva J. Dawn notes, the church can step to the fore. "Since the powers' sovereignty has been broken and a limit has been set to their working, the Church, clothed in God's armor, is the sign and the promise of their ultimate and total defeat."[8] Thus it is the church's time. In a moment of upheaval, marked by the atmospherics of fear, worry, and anxiety, we may flinch. But if we open our eyes we will see that the church faces some incredible opportunities. The Lord has defeated our foes. Look into the future and they are bowing before Him. Knowing this, we can charge ahead.

CHAPTER 11

TRANSGRESSING BOUNDARIES

As we have learned so far, our cultural myths are failing us. Therefore, to live as a Christian in this age, one thing we must do is serve as truth tellers, not merely in the sense of proclaiming the truth of God's Word, but debunking myths with our very lives—peeling back the smokescreen that blinds our lost neighbors. We must trespass into the wild holy and show the world that life is there.

Missiologist Lesslie Newbigin notes that "a community of people that, in the midst of all the pain and sorrow and wickedness of the world, is continually praising God is the first obvious result of living by another story than the one our world lives by."[1] In a time marked by the fleshiness, fatigue, and fear that secularism produces when churches have fallen back into the elemental forces, Newbigin points out that it is "our duty to pray for the reviving work of the Holy Spirit to kindle into flame the embers that are always there." For where there is a Spirit, there will be praise and joy, elements that are luminous in our world, that reach further than a viral tweet and speak louder than a marketing campaign. The Spirit leads not just to joy and praise but also love. Not the soppy, soapy reduction, recycled in greeting cards and made-for-television romances, but the blood-and-guts love that emerges from Calvary—the self-denying love that crosses the borders and barriers erected in our world against God and others and obliterates flesh and fallacy.

In this endeavor Peter Leithart counsels us that "like Jesus, we need to identify the pressure points, the sacred boundaries on which the modern cosmos is built, and then find ways to transgress those boundaries. We need places to eat with sinners, to eat with one another."[2] Such a boundary-breaking love will transgress the barriers the world erects, and desacralize the myths that powers propagate. It will look nothing like the impulses of modernity, of contemporary leftism to tear down all institutions, traditions, and conventions.

Following Leithart's counsel, I want to imagine in this chapter what it might look like to transgress modern sacred boundaries in the liberating love of Christ. Such transgressions are at once a departure from and critique of the holy places where our neighbors worship. Some transgressions will critique the quests for unlimited freedom that attempt to move beyond God's creational order into a post-Christian reengineering of culture. Others will critique the nature of our daily rhythms, and whether they are conducive to Christian discipleship. F. F. Bruce notes that Paul, preaching the gospel in pagan territory, had to "deal with some converts from paganism who misinterpreted gospel freedom to mean license to do whatever they chose, to indulge their old propensities unchecked."[3] In the same way, both Christians and our post-Christian society can reach for utopia by attempting to tear down structures and institutions, such as traditional notions of gender, sexuality, and family. But in this they rebel against the grain of God's created order. The question then becomes, which boundary promises true flourishing?

History has shown that contemporary crusades to deconstruct gender and neutralize the family unit—to undo the creational order—are ultimately futile. For example, the Soviets abandoned their attempts to destroy marriage and the family unit by the early 1930s as the devastating social effects of their policy became apparent when birth rates plummeted and the social fabric unraveled.[4] Their social engineering seemed to tinker with something far beyond their control or understanding, like they were rewiring their society in the dark, attempting to move beyond boundaries woven into the fabric of creation.

When it comes to social structures and identity, biblical faith actually takes a more radical path. Paul notes that there is no longer male or female, Gentile or Jew, in the church, yet at the same time affirms the creational order. Male and female still exists according to Scripture. The separations we find in the creation account of Genesis are still at play in this age. The same is true for cultures and nations. While we are encouraged to move beyond the elemental forces of cultural division, Scripture still maintains cultural distinction. In the book of Revelation, every tribe, tongue, and nation bring their glory and honor to God in the New Jerusalem. Humans are fallen yet created in the image of God. The nations are the same in that way, and just as God intends redemption for us, He intends to redeem the nations. He sends His disciples to the nations to bring them the light of the gospel. Those who once rebelled against God's chains, at the conclusion of Revelation honor God, are now guided by His light.

We are not at the culmination of history. We are close, but the New Jerusalem in all its glory has not descended among us. Understanding that we are in the latter days, the limitations that we face are turned on their head, no longer oppressing but used to turn us toward God. Their contours are used to disciple us, aid us in our battle against the flesh. This is true for us as individuals, but also as individuals who exist in social worlds, networks, communities and nations. The limitations that we face at a cultural level, when reframed in the battle between Spirit and flesh, can be turned to honor God and kill the flesh in us.

One example can be found in our contemporary attitude toward children. To a culture built on radical individualism, and the achievement culture, which says that the self can have it all, children and the complications and responsibilities they bring limit us. We now reel from this reality, causing a demographic disaster in the future of the West as our fertility rates plummet to unsustainable levels. Others who have children do so through the prism of it being a kind of restrictive punishment. Yet families, and the restrictions and limitations they bring, can be great aids in the battle against flesh.

Herman Bavinck reframes the limitations of family life, which many contemporary parents struggle with. He shows how family helps with discipleship, noting that children "develop within their parents an entire cluster of virtues." These virtues are developed through limitations, for family "exerts a reforming power upon the parents . . . Children place restraints upon ambitions." The flesh of self-actualization is held back by the creational order, pushing us toward life in the Spirit. "The family transforms ambition into service, miserliness into munificence, the weak into the strong, cowards into heroes, coarse fathers into mild lambs, tenderhearted mothers into ferocious lionesses."[5] The brilliance of Christianity is turning our challenges into the gold of a Christlike character. The rhythms and realities of human life are transformed into discipleship resources.

Unlike the broad-brushstroke thought of our day, Christianity carries great nuance, pushing us toward equality and justice while affirming the creational order. For example, Scripture speaks to those who may feel outside the creational order. In Acts the apostle Philip encounters an Ethiopian eunuch reading the book of Isaiah. Philip leads the African envoy to Christ. The eunuch crosses the border of baptism and enters the church. Much has been rightly made of the eunuch's reading of Isaiah, a book filled with prophecies concerning the coming Messiah, for indeed the eunuch was waiting for this Christ. But there is an element of Isaiah that many miss, of probable profound importance to the eunuch. This man was likely castrated to be a kind of priest, not of a god but of a royal house. His masculinity was removed to prevent a fleshly and illicit congress with a queen. Putting him in a gender grey space neutralized him as a threat. As he passed beautiful women, loving married couples, and happy families, he would always feel distant, always waiting for a marriage that can never come.

He was scarred and castrated by the elemental forces.

Contemporary identity politics would attempt to rectify this situation with the politics of recognition, encouraged to celebrate their eunuch-ness, while encouraging others to downplay the significance of genitalia, so as not to offend. However, the eunuch was looking for something deeper. For in the book of Isaiah, the prophet conveys a specific promise to eunuchs:

> "Don't let the eunuchs say, 'I'm a dried-up tree with no children and no future.' For this is what the LORD says: I will bless those eunuchs who keep my Sabbath days holy and who choose to do what pleases me and commit their lives to me. I will give them—within the walls of my house—a memorial and a name far greater than sons and daughters could give. For the name I give them is an everlasting one. It will never disappear!" (Isa. 56:3–5 NLT)

Instead of fear and loss, the eunuch receives something greater—an everlasting name. In the gospel of John, this particular eunuch becomes a father—not of children, but of the church of an entire continent. Today in Africa, a land filled with millions living out a vibrant Christian faith, Christians can look back to this first African Christian who found in his Messiah something greater than marriage.

Faith offers us not the simplistic contemporary solutions of the West, but rather grace-filled nuances. Marriage and family life push us toward God—away from the radical individualism of today and toward the servanthood of Christ. For others, celibacy and abstinence can be a rebellion against the culture of sexual modernity, which elevates intercourse beyond its created station. Celibacy becomes a redemptive protest against a culture that places the orgasm as the highest individual good. Instead, the biblical vision of abstinence leads to an infilling of God. The content virgin testifies to this truth: *God satisfies. He is enough.*

Further, the Christian church allows people on all places of the family spectrum—married, never-married, celibate, infertile—to be part of a family. As Friedrich Von Hugel says, "There are two poles within the Church . . . The pole of renouncing . . . and the domestic pole—the married people who go whole into things. We need them both to make Christianity and the Church very wide, very deep and inclusive."[6] *Thus the church will not be carriers of recognition politics, which seeks to affirm people in the way they wish to be affirmed.* The church affirms that the identities we devise apart from God are the problem—that all have sinned and fallen short of the glory of God, that we like sheep have gone astray. The church, rather than reinforcing our sinful identities with recognition politics, gives the deepest recognition possible: that each person is made in the image of God, is truly seen and known by the Creator of the universe, and can be adopted into His family regardless of the identities they used to hold. The gospel says, "You are more than your orientation, experience of gender, marital status, or societal role. You are a child of God." This frees us from holding those descriptors as identities. We don't have to enforce the border of social identity, because we aren't behind it. We're not vulnerable to its attack.

The elemental powers of social identity have skewed our

self-understanding. They have muddied our minds and hearts. The gospel, refusing to merely massage our self-esteem and confidence, gets down to the bone. The eyes of Christ see into the very marrow of our hearts, where even we are afraid to go. He sees everything we hate about ourselves, our deepest shames and fears, our faults and failures, and there He whispers to us, "You are loved." He tells us that despite all of our rebellion, all our fleshly defenses, all our demented strivings, there is hope. For He has taken all of it in His own body upon the cross in absolute, utter, bloody, sacrificial love. And He left it there (Col. 2:14). This sparkling concept of grace, this pure givenness that undermines fleshly achievement, this grace going out to call sinners home—it is the greatest transgressive force in the universe. Requiring us to transgress our own will, to surrender our fleshly pretensions, it offers the freedom we all sing for.

TECHNOLOGY AND THE LOST ART OF LIVEDNESS

Another border to transgress is the border erected by emerging technologies between life and our online, disembodied lives. That Christianity could have anything to say about our approach to technology may seem legalistic at first, but an essential dimension of following Christ is participating in His body, and this is a flesh-and-blood existence.

One of the most beautiful aspects of Christianity is that the incredible truth that Christ saves us in His body of flesh by the Spirit is not something we apprehend only spiritually. We meditate on it, we receive it, we build our lives on it, yes, but we can also have dinner with it. I'm talking here about the church.

The church is the body of Christ. Local assemblies are designed to bear witness to Him—to be His hands and feet. As Christ is love and lives His life in the Spirit, so the church is love and lives its life in the Spirit. "Such a community is the primary hermeneutic of the gospel," declares Newbigin, for "all the statistical evidence goes to show that those within our secularized societies who are being drawn out of unbelief to faith in Christ say that they were drawn through the friendship of a local congregation."[7] *Just as the temple was the magnet people were drawn to, the life of the Spirit lived in the temple "of a collective body" becomes magnetic itself.* Faithfully proclaiming Christ and patterning our lives after Him—imitating His love, embodying His teachings, inviting outsiders to the table—this is how the world sees Christ.

The very lived nature of Christian communal life increasingly becomes rare in the twenty-first-century world, for livedness is downplayed in our culture. The organs of power increasingly communicate to us through the digital world. We rarely meet politicians; rather, we see their digitalized forms daily. We do not experience the influence of celebrities, sports stars, and the titans of business in an enfleshed form. Rather, to experience their impact we must consume images and information about them via the Internet or television. Less and less do we get to know our local bank teller, find out how their kids are, or chat with the cashier in our favorite store. Such interactions now hover in digital form on our screens, ensconced in a part of our consciousness.

One day, after entering this online consciousness to consume the news, I was confronted with a social landscape stretched to the breaking point. Divisions between left and right, angry tweets, indignant punditry, terrorism, tensions over the place of Islam in the West. Putting down my iPad and heading out the door to pick up my daughter from school, I reenter the lived world.

There I feel awareness of my body moving, my legs stretching as I walk down the hill. The sun warms the back of my neck. Entering the school, before me runs the gamut of Western multiculturalism. A myriad of different ethnicities and religions, all acting in a wonderfully mundane ballet of wiping kids' noses, dragging along toddlers, holding basketballs and footballs under their arms, lugging scooters and schoolbags. Instead of a fractious, fragmented, fiery online reality, there is calm, peace, a pleasant parallel universe. Friendly nods, waves of recognition, the hum of small talk.

I watch a young mum arrive, holding in her arms a newborn baby. Smiles break out. Quickly she is surrounded by a handful of other mothers, all beaming at the new arrival, kisses and hugs of congratulations are exchanged. Women in tank tops and yoga pants, some in jeans and tattoos, others in multicolored Islamic scarves. There is no tension, no arguments, no flaming tweets, just a group of humans, interacting face-to-face as we have always interacted. United in the small bandwidth of mundane activities humans have always engaged in. This is the real world. This is the enfleshed world.

Despite all of the adulation given to the digital landscape, despite its increasing incursion into our lives, we still live in the enfleshed, ordinary world. Just look how we crane our necks, uncomfortably walk with our gaze set on our screens, commune with sofa and flat screen. It is not our home, but a temporary place of residence for our attentions, a distraction, an echo chamber of opinions and vain words.

At risk of seeming to tell a sentimental story in which a newborn baby unites humanity and undoes all of the problems I have outlined in this book, I wish to clarify my point. We live most of our lives in the real world. We live part of our lives in the feverish, hovering space of the digital world. Such a world can overwhelm us with its immersive power, leaving us ill-equipped for the reality of livedness. The influence of the online world, with all of its divisions and distractions, can lead us even as believers to take it as normative. Fretting and fearing at our cultural turn. However, there is a hope that many have missed. *Christians, formed by the church, shaped by its relational rhythms, abiding with Christ, fighting flesh and living in the Spirit, are built for the real world.* It is the realm in which the church flourishes and creates community with a heavenly destination.

The church provides good news. Re-centering life around the worship of God, it is the perfect environment for human flourishing. It gives needed, but also tough, medicine for those formed and shaped by the contours of our digitized, consumer-driven world. For the change we are living through wrought by social media and the digital world is a technological one, yet it is shaped by an ideology, a dogma of techno utopianism.

The initial designer of the Internet, Tim Berners-Lee, states that the web is not so much a technological invention but a social one. It was a platform to create social change, one whose supporting pillars were radical individualism, mystical faith in the power of technology and innovation, and the Californian counterculture's resistance to authority, which is soaked deep in the soil beneath the industrial parks of Silicon Valley.

The original visionaries of our online worlds, observes tech commentator Andrew Keen, "imported the sixties' disruptive libertarianism, its rejection of hierarchy and authority, its infatuation with openness, transparency and personal authenticity, and its global communitarianism into the culture of what has become known as 'cyberspace.' Their vision was to unite all human beings in a global network linked by computers."[8] This vision is a digital non-place. It believes that digital networks and online worlds can offer us community and connection while preserving our individual autonomy and freedom. It is this *ideology*, not the technology itself, which does the damage to our psychological, social, and spiritual selves.

The anxiety that hums like a computer in the background of our contemporary lives alerts us—not to the inherent danger in technology—but rather the inability of digital networks to deliver human flourishing and the deep connection for which the human soul desires. Yes, the new digital landscape has delivered handy ways to connect, as well as unparalleled access to information. Yet its technological utopianism, now monetized and designed to elicit consumer desires at a neurological level, has profoundly formed us. To move from the pure "livedness" of this digital, consumeristic, constantly connected state of being, into the pure "livedness" of the church, can be a jarring one. The gospel invitation into the community of discipleship, which is the church, can seem far from good news. It can feel like a cold shower.

For a hyperspeed culture of connectivity, the slow and

steady pace of discipleship can seem glacial. The silences and pauses of the Christian life, the waiting and abiding, can seem deafening. A life defined by the holy Word, the preached Word, and the Word made flesh, can seem alien in the age of the image, archaic compared to omnipresent screens, online shopping, and continual scrolling. For those shaped by digital silos of the likeminded and the social clustering facilitated by the algorithms of tech giants, encountering the body of Christ—consisting of many parts, made up of people not like us—can be a shock. The intensification of radical individualism created by our digital age, in which individuals fold into themselves as they bend over the screen of their smartphone, means that the life of discipleship, and the battle against flesh, is a battle against the self. All who come to Christ must lay their lives down before Christ, regardless of the particularities of the epoch and culture they find themselves in. Our age is no different. But our phones train us not to do this.

Over half a century ago the Christian statesman and Methodist missionary E. Stanley Jones wrote of sharing his faith with a smart Soviet actress, a communist committed to a materialist worldview. Suspicious of the supernatural, spiritual nature of Christianity, the Russian actress mocked Jones as weak. In her estimation he was a religious man, and religion was for those who needed a crutch in life. Jones countered that Christian faith was not a crutch, but rather a vision of life devoted to selflessness, a sacrificial path built around serving God and others. Such an altruistic tack, however, did nothing to impress or sway the young woman. To her, the contours of the kingdom of God and the way of faith described by Jones were simply disconnected from real life. They were a pure and unworkable idealism. Dismissively, she bid Jones farewell and left the conversation stating that she was a realist.

Raised on the concreteness of Soviet doctrine, faith appeared to her as an ideal, which existed on a plane of thought thousands of feet above the ground of reality and livedness. Her conscious had been trained under Soviet cultural formation. Her communist education shaped her to have intellectual objections to the idea that Christian faith could be connected to actual lived human life and the betterment of human society.

Increasingly I realize that as a pastor I find myself in a similar predicament to Jones, albeit with some key differences. Jones encountered in the communist actress someone with an explicit understanding of why they believed that Christianity could not apply to real life. In the secular environments where we find ourselves, this disbelief in the truth of Christ's call to holy living, to the transformational nature of faith, is not dismissed explicitly. Rather, it creates a cognitive dissonance between the truth of the gospel and the gospel of our age. It says that human flourishing happens within boundaries—within a shared identity and its necessary attending commitments. That is, as a Christian, you obey the Lord and submit to other Christians in love and humility. It is not you first. You are limited. You are bound. And in this there is freedom.

But our culture says, "Not so." Whether the boundaries are autonomy of sexual expression or the freedoms of digital life—or any other boundary—to transgress them is to impede on freedom. To threaten human flourishing. Flourishing occurs in non-places, where you decide your own destiny, where you live unbridled by commitments—by "restrictions," the new swear word of the twenty-first century.

I believe this cognitive dissonance, this gap between the promises of twenty-first-century globalized culture and what it actually delivers, is behind much of our epidemic of anxiety. The elemental powers are a smokescreen keeping us from knowing life as it should be. Therefore we must next turn to a major theme of the Christian life—life in exile—and its deep relevance to our strange days.

CHAPTER 12

WHAT KIND OF EXILE
IS THIS?

Much of contemporary Christian resources on discipleship, ministry, and mission are centered on responding
to a fast-fading reality. So many write, preach, and teach against
a cultural Christianity high on piety, low on practice, which
separated itself from the world, derided as too heavenly to be
any earthly good. For many in past generations the distance
between the culture of the Christianity of their youth, or their
parents' youth, or of the church they encounter in other places,
and the reality of faith they encounter in Scripture, creates
a deep sense of dissatisfaction. This dissatisfaction, and the
desire to define one's faith and church practice against such
unbiblical models of Christian expression, can operate like the
gravitational pull of a nearby moon, hidden in the darkness
but still influencing with an invisible force. A pull that has the
potential to warp not only our current practice, but cause us to
misread our current reality.

As the distance between conventional forms of evangelical

Christianity and a rapidly secularizing Western culture grew, so did the desire to model and practice a faith that did not unthinkingly reject culture completely, or wall itself off in Christianized social enclaves. New approaches to cultural interface were explored. The paradigm of missiology was adopted. The lessons learned by missionaries in the two-thirds world were brought back to Western contexts, the practice of contextualization increasingly shaping local ministry. Best practices from the business and marketing fields were employed. As cultural Christianity appeared to fade, church leaders started speaking of a new divide: the gap between Christianity and—whatever you wanted to call it: modernity, secularism, post-modernity, post-Christianity—the social force that was moving away from the West's cultural roots. As the reality of this situation grew, alongside a rediscovery of a missional posture, the Old Testament language of exile gained new resonance.

In the biblical story, the exile has several dimensions. It refers to the Babylonian and Assyrian conquest of Judah and Israel, respectively, and to the devastation wrought upon Jerusalem and the temple—the tearing out of Israel's very heart. It refers also to the cultural displacement of those who were taken away to a foreign city, where they had to practice their faith in a foreign place, forever surrounded by powerful and seductive idols. There, God's people walked a tightrope between faithfulness and cultural engagement, wondering if He would return to them with mercy.

These dimensions seemed to offer analogies to Western Christianity at the end of the twentieth century and into the beginning of the twenty-first. The mourning, the sense of lostness the people of God felt at the destruction of their land, the cultural dislocation—it seemed to gel with the passing of Christendom, the displacement of Christianity from the Western imagination, and the new social arrangement the church found itself in.

The analogy of exile not only seemed to offer solace, but also hope. The prophet Jeremiah, himself an exile in Babylon, encouraged the Jews in exile in Babylon with these words from God:

> "Build houses and settle down; plant gardens and eat
> what they produce. Marry and have sons and daughters;
> find wives for your sons and give your daughters in
> marriage, so that they too may have sons and daughters.
> Increase in number there; do not decrease. Also, seek
> the peace and prosperity of the city to which I have
> carried you into exile. Pray to the LORD for it, because if
> it prospers, you too will prosper." (Jer. 29:5–7 NIV)

This has become a keystone passage for many, including me, in order to navigate our current cultural challenges.

However, as Christian exegesis of Scripture informs us, the Hebrew Scriptures of the Old Testament must be read through the lens of Christ: His ministry, death, and resurrection. There is nothing wrong with applying Jeremiah's encouragement to our current situation, but without an application of how Christ's work has radically changed the essence of history and the cosmos, we can drift into subtle errors. Not a dramatic theological error, nor a devastating heresy, but a nuance that can work against the flourishing of our ministry, mission, and discipleship. In this chapter, I compare two views of our exile, outlining some issues with a pre-Christ view and calling us instead to a post-ascension view.

PRE-CHRIST EXILE

There are two dangers to applying Jeremiah's exilic advice without a Christological lens. The first is that we can mistakenly adopt a missional practice based on a popular but wrong idea: that the church is engaged in a culture war with secular society. The cultural force is against the church, but through rigorous cultural engagement we can flourish as the culture around us flourishes. No longer do we even necessarily expect to capture the culture for Christ, but instead at least enjoy the fruits of our secularized culture, while doggedly clinging to faith.

It is worth noting that the popularity of viewing our current cultural predicament through the lens of exile grew during the "end of history" phase in the decades that followed the fall of the Berlin Wall, where peace, prosperity, possibility, and progressivism appeared triumphant. Thus, models of cultural engagement, rightly instigated, could also implicitly communicate the message that one could flourish in exile, enjoying all the fruits of society. In other words, the way to be comfortable as a Christian is to make culture more Christian.

It seems to me, though, that this approach is fading. Instead, we have veered into another danger: we settle in with culture to try and influence it for Christ. We contextualize so heavily that we dishonor—usually subtly and unknowingly—the biblical distinctions between the church and the world.

Contemporary pastors can probably resonate with this a

good deal, particularly those pastoring people in their forties who live in increasingly secular environments, like cities. Unlike in the past, or parts of the West where cultural Christianity still holds sway, they are not ministering to cultural Christians averse to engagement with the world. Rather, leaders of Bible-based, orthodox churches now find themselves leading congregations where the world is sitting right in their pews.

Among many professed disciples—especially young ones—cultural values are swallowed up whole. Take sexuality, for example. The sexual revolution has incredibly altered the social landscape of contemporary Christian community and practice. Pornography use is rampant among males and a growing and significant percentage of females. Sexual activity among unmarried singles is normative, and digital apps like Tinder are commonly used to facilitate casual sexual encounters. An understanding of how to find a spouse, or even how to date as a Christian, is disappearing in our commitment-averse culture. The contemporary pastor leads a church where many will no longer marry, not because of desire to embrace biblical celibacy, but because the entire social mechanism that facilitates match-making for the purpose of lifelong covenantal relationships is buckling under the pressure of the achievement society. Where the body is not rejected by a too-heavenly spirituality, but rather is virtually worshiped, seen as a route to happiness and fulfillment. Where relationships, commitment, and responsibility are interpreted through the lens of consumerism and radical individualism. They are impediments, not gifts. And so a generation of Christians is saying no to something God designed in part for their sanctification, opting instead for continued unbridled autonomy. (And they are seeing that autonomy often comes with loneliness.)

Emotional health also seems to be deteriorating. The contemporary congregation is one where anxiety is widespread, in many cases experienced by the majority. Byung-Chul Han attributes our contemporary epidemic of anxiety—not just within the church, but generally—to the cultural shift from disciplinary culture to achievement culture, which I discussed earlier. In the former, a set system of rules and structures ensured that corporate responsibility restrained and directed individual desires and dysfunctions. Now, however, external discipline is reduced to a bare minimum, and the individual is not told what he or she cannot do, but rather all they can do. The individual swims in a sea of images and information all proclaiming he or she can be all things. Prohibitions are replaced with endless possibility. For the follower of Jesus living and being shaped by the achievement culture, filled with potential and promised pleasures, a unique discipleship challenge emerges: the formational patterns of society run roughshod against the gospel's call to self-renunciation.

Why, despite all the advances in church ministry practices, the embrace of cutting-edge technology, the wealth of resources available on the web, are we seeing degradation in the moral and spiritual climate of congregations? Why has the church failed to address the epidemic of anxiety and depression in our culture, the distance between the promises of consumer culture and the reality of life, and the emotional fragility and lack of resilience created by the self-esteem ethos? Because the church has subtly reinforced that very self-esteem ethos. It has propagated the patterns of achievement society and non-places. To put it bluntly, the church has become a marketing firm for Jesus.

Consumer culture is replete with advertisements featuring sandaled feet on sandy beaches, lone and toned hikers stretching their arms before natural vistas, communal dinners on wooden tables filled with groupings of attractive young adults, smiling as they relax in their smart casual clothes woven from natural fibers. The Danish concept of *hygge*—roughly translated as *coziness*—in which tight groups of friends enjoy the simple pleasure of cocooning around a meal, has now become a full-blown marketing phenomenon. One used to sell all kinds of products, while implicitly promising to keep the increasingly frightening outside world at bay. Thus we can (and I have flown close to this error myself in the past) preach the lived reality of the Christian faith as something akin to such a vision. The grandeur of Christ's kingship and glorious kingdom reduced to less conspicuous consumption, physical and emotional well-being, community engagement and simple pleasures. A faith to flourish in exile, but minus Jesus' call to repentance and relinquishment. A broad path that leads not to the cross but to disappointment, anxiety, and paralysis.

Presenting faith in this way attempts to offer a way out of the pressures of achievement culture while unconsciously still adhering to its essential structures. It can commit the error of presenting the kingdom of God as an alternative social arrangement to be constructed in the face of our powerful society of materialism filled with isolation and the breakdown of community. Yet it fails to address the core issues of self-absorption and the tyranny of emotionalism that is enabled by the achieve-

ment society, which cause us to remain as infants, tossed back
and forth by the waves as Paul warned in Ephesians. So not
only does it fail to save those drowning in self-absorption, it
unknowingly keeps their heads underwater.

To use biblical language, the achievement society offers us
the promise of unlimited options and personal potential, but
ignores the reality of sin and the flesh. Attempts to communicate Christian truth increasingly run awry because the promise
of kingdom living, abundant life, and exilic flourishing can
sound a lot like having it all—deep friendships, satisfying mar-
riages, simple rewarding lifestyles, communion with nature,
wellness of mind and body. If we are not careful, discipleship
and faith can thus become overwritten by the achievement society, in which unlimited potential is promised, earthly expectations are inflated, and repentance is ignored.

Undoubtedly there is nothing wrong with using the language
of exile to describe our current missional context. The New
Testament reaches back into the exilic Scriptures of the Old
Testament and applies them to the reality of the early church.
There is also no sin in engaging with culture, with desiring
the peace, prosperity, and flourishing of your city. However, the
crisis of discipleship, the way in which the cultural script of
the achievement society has so deeply shaped the inner world
and life of our emerging generations, is evidence that something
is missing.

A SECOND EXILE

We are not in exile in the same way Israel was while living in
Babylon. Babylon was a culture in the sway of the elemental

forces, its entire culture built around a specific form of religious worship. Israel was the same, but shaped by temple and Torah, guided by God. The kingdom of God, still a hidden secret, was only hinted at, experienced in glimpses. The Messiah, the coming King hoped for, pined for, and prayed for, had not yet arrived. The Spirit of God, falling at times, but only on some, was sporadic and temporary in His visitations. The fundamental building blocks of the universe, the elemental forces, had not changed.

With Christ's appearing, everything changed. The Messiah had come. The promises of the prophets had been fulfilled. The kingdom was now an open secret. The Spirit, now a constant guide and companion, became available to all who would bend their knee to Christ. The fundamental elements of the universe had irrevocably been changed. No longer is the temple the center of the biblical universe. No longer do the people of God pine for the Shekinah glory to return to the temple. Instead, as Paul writes to the church in Ephesus, the people of God, filled with the Spirit, have Christ as their cornerstone. God's household, of which Christians are members, "rises to become a holy temple in the Lord . . . a dwelling in which God lives by his Spirit" (Eph. 2:21–22 NIV).

This is a post-elemental forces faith. Thus exile cannot be the same. We cannot simply sit back and wait for God to end our cultural exile, aiming to flourish. The victory is won, the game has changed. A new era is here. As heavenly citizens we exist in a kind of exile, but in a different epoch, thus deserving of a different missional posture. Yes, we are called to flourish, but we are called also into a spiritual war against the powers and principalities, now humiliated on the cross by Christ. There is a key nuance here: flourishing needs a fight against the flesh. We find meaning not in the promises of the achievement culture, or the mirage of the "end of history," but in the battle against that which is not God, a conflict that takes on a personal dimension as we battle the flesh within.

A hint of this different kind of exile is found in the teachings of the medieval Christian author Thomas à Kempis, who counsels, "It is good for us to encounter troubles and adversities from time to time, for trouble often compels a man to search his own heart. It reminds him that he is an exile here, and that he can put his trust in nothing in this world."[1] This is a different exile, not an exile from place but from the world. History has fundamentally altered and now slants toward its fulfillment in Christ's uniting of heaven and earth at the end of the age. This is an exile with an eternal dimension.

After the cross, a new border is erected in the world, between the flesh, which is passing and which resists God, and the Spirit, which reflects God. A time in which Christ has won the ultimate victory upon the cross, but the forces that oppose God wage their insurgency before His return. Their insurgency will fail, yet it still carries the potential to do great damage. Sin is still active in the world, we live in the damage wrought by the flesh upon our social fabric, we live with the internal damage done by the flesh upon ourselves. The damage done by sin in our world means that we cannot have it all. Salvation yes, but all earthly benefits no. The kingdom is not a means of getting around this, of having fully satisfying lives in which we get to feast from the full fruit of earthly creation while around us sin destroys and damages. The earth still groans, waiting for release from the effects of sin. It waits for its exile to end, for history to reach its end. The limitations, blockages, and difficulties of this exile point us toward God, reminding us that our only solace can be found in Him.

Understanding our life as an ongoing exile, in which limitations and difficulties point us back to God, flies in the face of much of our cultural formation. For our achievement culture at its core, powered by the rise of therapy as a kind of secular religion, has elevated feelings as the peak of human flourishing. The greatest good is to feel good. As cultural critic Edwin Schur notes, "Potential and growth are thought of and talked about in strictly personal terms. Their presence or absence is determined in or through the individual's own feelings."[2] The contemporary life script of the achievement culture is to arrange a life that delivers constant pleasurable feelings, to keep the social and psychic borders up, to keep negative feelings outside.

When positive emotions become the pinnacle of personal growth, a tyranny of feelings is quickly established. Compounded by the belief, communicated from Disney children's movies to self-help literature, that a life free of negative feelings and painful emotions is eminently possible. This belief is confirmed by contemporary parenting styles and dominant educational practices that insulate the young from the painful realities of life, the sting of disappointments and consequences, and the limiting reality of a broken creation. Thus when limitations and difficulties are encountered in early adulthood, faith can be approached as a panacea to the experience of negative feelings. As something that will assist the individual in the achievement of ever greater levels of positive and rewarding feelings.

However, life in the Spirit, as described by the New Testament, is a very different proposition than the accruing of positive emotions and feelings. God's salvation plan is a far broader canvas than the simple inflating of individual emotions. Instead our eternal exile aligns us with the reality of the kingdom of God in a profound way.

The kingdom is the area under the rule and reign of God. We do not build this reign, instead we submit to it. "Whether men 'receive' that rule is another question," E. Stanley Jones cautions. "If they do not receive it, then all the worse for them, for the kingdom then operates in self-frustration and self-destruction. Men hurt themselves if they do not receive the kingdom."[3] Jones's insight is a powerful one. The kingdom is both good news and bad news. Good news to those who grasp their own wretchedness and spiritual need. Bad news to those who wish to preserve their own individual autonomy. Observing Jesus' teaching in the Gospels we see again and again that those who grasp their own weakness, who come to the end of themselves, who realize their own limitations, are the ones who are close to the kingdom. Those who understand and experience the exile of this time find themselves close to the kingdom.

We see this powerfully in the story of the man oppressed by a legion of demons. This devastating oppression wracks him. He was both literally and spiritually in chains. The dark forces oppressing him had driven him into solitary places. A man overcome with pain, anxious, fearful, driven into a punishing loneliness. Delivered by Jesus, his neighbors in the region find him freed, dressed, at peace, sitting at Jesus' feet. This stunning good news, this gospel deliverance, this entry of a once tormented man into the kingdom of God is not met with cheers by his community. Instead Jesus is told to leave, the good news of the man's deliverance is received as bad news by those who live around him. This miracle overcomes them with fear, the outbreaking of the kingdom of God is viewed as a threat.

"God did not and does not come to the self-sufficient," writes R. Kent Hughes, noting that "Christianity began and always begins with a spirit of need—spiritual destitution."[4] Shaped by the achievement society, and the non-places of our world, which form us to believe an unlimited life is possible. Experiencing the gap between this promise and the reality of our lives, we can force ourselves to greater levels of exertion, or collapse into a fatigued funk, or cycle between both. Googling life hacks, or retreating into passivity, all while the anxiety grows within. Thus we can reach the end of ourselves, but instead of being close to the true kingdom of God we can recoil in fear, fearful of giving up our expectations, shaped by the achievement society. Instead of examining the validity of our own expectations, we live in the thrall of anxiety, illustrating the incompatibility of kingdom living with the life script of the achievement society.

During the Babylonian exile, the prophets warned the people of God not to succumb to the worship of idols, to bend their knee to foreign gods. The injunction against idol worship is still there in the New Testament; however, on the other side of the cross, it is not just idols, but heresies, deceitful philosophies, false teachers that the believer must be wary of. Now freed from the elemental forces, and experiencing the liberation of the gospel,

Paul warns the believers in Galatia to not "use your freedom to indulge the flesh" (Gal 5:13 NIV).

This is more than a simple descent into the realm of obvious sins such as lust and gluttony. This is a warning that, though freed from sin, the flesh must still be continually crucified. The flesh being any mindset, action, and attitude that is not led by the Spirit. Paul elucidates further: "So I say, walk by the Spirit, and you will not gratify the desires of the flesh. For the flesh desires what is contrary to the Spirit, and the Spirit what is contrary to the flesh. They are in conflict with each other, is that you are not to do whatever you want" (Gal 5:16–17 NIV). Living by the Spirit, then, in a world of flesh, is our exile. Our next and final chapter explores a biblical template for this kind of living.

CHAPTER 13

ON EARTH AS IT IS
IN HEAVEN

Once Christ, the eternal God incarnate, enters the temporal, He brings the life of the Trinity into clear view. Eternal secrets now spill into view. The divine dance between Father, Son, and Spirit, which hovered over the primordial waters, is now on display for those whose eyes have been opened. A fifteenth-century French illustration captures with great intrigue an interesting way to understand this divine relationship, picturing God the Father and Jesus the Son, seated and facing each other in a conversational pose. Between their faces with a wing in each mouth, the dove, representing the Holy Spirit. The Spirit the conversation, the relationship, the life between heavenly Father and divine Son.

Having completed His work on the cross, and having emerged from the tomb, Christ does not stay. Israel had been shaped for forty years in the wilderness before they could enter the Promised Land, and the resurrected Christ spends forty days shaping His disciples, not for a place, nor for a trans-local utopia, but instead for life in the Spirit. Soon He would depart because the Spirit, the guide, the Counselor must come. Those who followed Christ must now become Christlike, His body in the world. Christ had incarnated eternity into the world, lived the life of God within creation, now the church itself must incarnate life in the spirit in the world. Confronting the forces of darkness that bind humans in the world, crucifying the flesh, the way Jesus had on the cross. This was the post-exilic way after the elemental forces of the universe had fundamentally been changed.

The church has always borne witness to Christ's overthrow of elemental forces. And though it's a quiet revolution, it's a revolution nonetheless. Historian Peter Brown writes of the years in which the gospel initially spread and the early church grew. The period, known as late antiquity, saw "a vast and anxious activity in religion."[2] The traditional forms of religion, the elemental forces, which since time immemorial had provided solace, meaning, and guidance, had shockingly been rejected by the Christians. No other religion ever had such a removal of the distance between God and man. Christians have God living in them.

The kind of direct life of God, accessible by the Spirit, now seemed to drain life from the surrounding pagan religions built around the elemental forces. The new religious mood seemed to desire "a God with whom one could be alone; a God whose 'charge', as it were, had remained concentrated and personal rather than diffused in benign but profoundly impersonal ministrations to the universe at large . . . The new mood . . . appealed straight to the centre away from the subordinate gods of popular belief—to the One God Himself, as a figure of latent, unexpressed power."[3] Dissatisfaction with traditional religion grew, a desire for the kind of direct revelation, a hunger for the spiritual battle Christians fought, in which evil and the invisible dark forces behind creation were directly confronted.

Christians live life in the Spirit before a watching world. We are not called to retreat from the world, nor to embrace it, but to live on earth as it is in heaven. We are citizens of both, but our citizenry in heaven, being eternal, usurps and entirely alters our citizenry on earth. Our exile is life in the Spirit, but that spiritual life is exceedingly practical. In this chapter, I'll provide a brief sketch of this kind of life. How do we live lives of quiet, holy protest against the elemental forces? How do we transgress the boundaries of this world and give our neighbors a glimpse of the world to come?

THE ROAR OF QUIET LIVING

Paul, using words like those of Jeremiah to the Babylonian exiles, has this to say to believers in the early church about how to conduct themselves:

> Finally, then, brothers, we ask and urge you in the Lord Jesus, that as you received from us how you ought to walk and to please God, just as you are doing, that you do so more and more. For you know what instructions we gave you through the Lord Jesus. For this is the will of God, your sanctification: that you abstain from sexual immorality; that each one of you know how to control his own body in holiness and honor, not in

the passion of lust like the Gentiles who do not know God; that no one transgress and wrong his brother in this matter, because the Lord is an avenger in all these things, as we told you beforehand and solemnly warned you. For God has not called us for impurity, but in holiness. Therefore whoever disregards this, disregards not man but God, who gives his Holy Spirit to you.

Now concerning brotherly love you have no need for anyone to write to you, for you yourselves have been taught by God to love one another, for that indeed is what you are doing to all the brothers throughout Macedonia. But we urge you, brothers, to do this more and more, and to aspire to live quietly, and to mind your own affairs, and to work with your hands, as we instructed you, so that you may walk properly before outsiders and be dependent on no one. (1 Thess. 4:1–12 ESV)

I believe that though our current global moment is in so many ways different from the early church's, this kind of life is the way forward. To live ordinarily and quietly, work with our hands, embrace the rhythms and realities of daily life, is seemingly mundane. However, it is actually how we engage in the great spiritual battle against the flesh and the powers and principalities.

One could be fooled by such a quiet life, yet when tuned to a heavenly frequency, such a life resounds with a mighty roar. For it is a call to live as the church, a creative minority, who live in the world but experience it in a profoundly different way. A way shaped by redemptive dislocation. As a people called to be in the world but not of it, we gain a distance from the rest of the world. We no longer live according to the elemental forces. We refuse to bow to the lies and myths of the powers and principalities. This crucial distance, this vital dislocation the Christ follower experiences, sets our lives into new healing patterns.

Reframing Life as Discipleship

By choosing to follow Jesus and forsake all other gods, idols, and authorities, we take on a new identity. We are adopted, justified, and made new. We also take on the identity of a disciple. One who follows, mimics, and continues the master's work. To take on the identity of a disciple, we eschew other identities. We are no longer just one of the crowd.

As disciples, we cannot choose passivity, nor do it all under our own steam. Instead the disciple lives at a distance from the crowd, as well as a distance from his own flesh. A disciple lives under the lordship of Jesus, guided, counseled, and quickened by the Spirit. In the "peerarchy" of contemporary culture, where we look to our peers as the ultimate authority and guide of our behavior and values, entering a hall of mirrors, reflecting to each other a constructed, perfected self on social media, we choose to take a different path. Loving our peers, but not bowing to them. In the opinionocracy, in which we are told that all opinions are valid, and which has descended into a deafening echo chamber of never-ending voices, broadcasting into the wind, we choose to speak the Father's truth.

By following the way of the disciple, we choose the narrow path that leads to life. We cannot take our cues from what everyone else is doing. Life must be approached as a disciple. We must ask, "How do we approach social media as a disciple?" "How do I parent as a disciple?" "How do I date as a disciple?" "How do I use my money as a disciple?" This simple question, "How do I live as a disciple?" reframes the whole of one's life, sends one to the Scriptures to seek guidance, wisdom, and truth. Aware of our flesh, we become suspicious of our own motivations and desires, approaching them through the testing of prayer. The disciple realizes that he or she cannot live life in the Spirit alone—deep, life giving, accountable, guiding spiritual community is needed. The disciple is someone who understands that the life of the Spirit happens within the redemptive social environment of the church. The simple nuance of seeing oneself as a disciple, called by Christ for a greater good, changes everything. For disciples live out of a greater story.

Seeing the Whole Story

Humans have always told stories. Stories that do not just entertain but that inform, teach, and shape. Humans have always found meaning in the great sweeping narratives that inform who we are, why we are here, and where we are going. The "end of history" phase that followed the fall of Berlin Wall, as we have learned, was shaped by radical individualism, consumerism, and a self-esteem ethos. These factors, alongside a dominant philosophical trend of postmodernism which rejected the grand narratives which gave us meaning, saw the shrinking of our narratives to stories of self.

Unparalleled freedom allowed us to seemingly write our own scripts. However, as we have learned, the poverty of meaning found in such reduced narratives that begin and end with "me" has led many to seek larger stories, stories shaped by the elemental forces—to find meaning in nationalism, or the utopianism of globalism. Yet these stories are still too small for the gospel. The chaos and current of the world tear at them. Still shaped by the elemental forces, human in origin, they cannot contain the desire for eternity in the human heart. They are not vast enough; they strain under their own pressures and contradictions. The world is too large, too complex, buffeted by chaos, confusion, and evil. Our ideologies, our conspiracy theories, our religions cannot offer the viewpoint we need to truly understand the world.

The Christian stands apart from the world. We have been given access and insight to God's grand redemptive plan. We see the arc of history, we look back to the wonder of creation and the origins of our fall, we see the historical record of God's dogged love. We see the cross, the hinge of history. We see the obliteration of the fleshly elemental forces. The rise of a new formation of people living by the Spirit, the church. The history of Christian faithfulness and redemptive service and mission, alongside the people of God, at times falling back into the seductive arms of the elemental forces. We see the advance of the gospel, the breaking out of the kingdom, the evangelization of far flung nations. Crucially we see the true end of history, not achieved by liberal democracy, a reembrace of blood and soil, or via a technological-driven globalization, but by the return of Christ, who will unite heaven and earth. This view is achieved from the highest of mountains. It is a resource that transforms our daily lives, giving us the grandest narrative that reorientates what is important and what is simply passing.

The quiet life that Paul encourages us to live in his letter to the Thessalonians gains an incredible magnetism when it is lived in light of this great holy drama. It a resource, which can be salt and light for those around us with a limited view. Who fear the times, seduced by the sirens of the age, the personal anxiety of a reduced story of self, and the cultural fear brought by the battle of clashing and competing stories. The Christian who lives by the grand story in our strange days becomes like the men of Issachar "who understood the times and knew what Israel should do" (1 Chron. 12:32).

Seeing the whole story, we understand that our age is not as modern, unique, and progressive as it believes. Like all ages, it is shaped by the elemental forces. Even in its secularism it is thus ultimately religious. Thus with our heavenly viewpoint we can become interpreters of the age, godly guides, merchants of holy hope. Our age is an age of clashing stories. Do not underestimate the power of the story you carry within your heart, the gospel that drips with goodness. For when a community of people, called by Christ, living as the church, come together, something truly wonderful happens.

The Social Architecture of the Church

The Christian understands the church as a vital resource in fighting the flesh. As the borders go up, its common meal of communion reorients us around our primary identity as citizens of heaven. Communion reminds us of the freedom, the reality of grace given to broken sinners, the ultimate social equalizing force. Yet at the same time, the commitment that church requires bites deep into our flesh, pulling us back from running into a dangerous freedom. In our contemporary culture, set around the needs of the individual, in which we pick and choose where to spend our time at our leisure, where formed as consumers we give but expect in return, the social architecture of the church reorients us away from a fleshly obsession on self. To be a truly redemptive force, a church needs the commitment of its individual members—those who shape their lives around its rhythms and calendar, who restrict their options and choose instead to serve the bride of Christ.

The small commitment of regular attendance grows into the commitment of loving brothers and sisters in Christ, which blossoms into the service of those outside the church, love of neighbor in sharing of good news and seeking of mercy and justice. The opposite of the works of the flesh, Paul reminds us in Galatians, is the fruit of the Spirit: "Love, joy, peace, patience, kindness, goodness, faith, gentleness, self-control" (Gal. 5:22–23). This fruit cannot be bought, or downloaded; instead it emerges from an inner life, shaped by the reality of fighting the flesh, of living by the Spirit in the church. It grows as it is sown—lovingly, carefully, tenderly, painstakingly, slowly. It is a shared crop, the result of imperfect people walking together toward Christlikeness.

The church, in our strange days, needs to be embedded in the soil in which it finds itself, speaking the local language and reflecting its community. Yet it cannot give into its community's myths, most pressingly the myth of the self as god. We need effective communication, eliminating unnecessary and unessential barricades on the way to the cross, yet we must also realize that we cannot lower the bar in order to leave the flesh unchallenged. For such a church, as Paul explains in Ephesians, is a witness, not just to her neighbors, but as an example of God's manifold wisdom to the powers and principalities of the heavenly realms (Eph. 3:10–11).

Freedom, Self, and Slavery

A life lived as a disciple, born out of God's grand narrative, shaped within the people of God, fighting the flesh, is a powerfully magnetic force. Freed from being a slave to the elemental forces, standing firm so as not to return to them. No longer must we sacrifice at the temple. Instead, life in the spirit, our freedom from the elemental forces, leads us to offer our lives as "living sacrifices, holy and pleasing to God," our true and proper worship (Rom. 12:1). No longer shaped by the formational mechanisms of the world, we discover through life in the spirit and the battle against flesh, "the renewing of your mind," a deep change as our lives come into alignment with God's will. The fear, the anxiety, the outrage, the virtue signaling, the desire for borders, of the transgression of smashing borders in one's own strength, gives way to being able to "discern what is the good, pleasing, and perfect will of God" (Rom. 12:2). By disobeying ourselves and obeying God we no longer march to the futile drumbeat of the inflated self. We do not boast of self, shaping a shiny, outer life, while our inner world lies broken. Instead we boast only of Christ.

Even when difficulties come, when suffering visits us, when we "are hard pressed on every side, but not crushed; perplexed, but not in despair; persecuted, but not abandoned; struck down, but not destroyed. We always carry around in our body the death of Jesus, so that the life of Jesus may also be revealed in our body" (2 Cor. 4:8–10 NIV). Suffering and pain, loss and grief—those things we fear, which we build our literal and symbolic borders to protect ourselves from, do not overcome a life lived in the Spirit. For when we are weak we are strong

(2 Cor. 12:10). Christ's power is made perfect in weakness. So instead of boasting of self, of building great temples to our own greatness, of constructing walls to keep that which we cannot control out, we live a life that is strong in God, when we are weak. Such a life moves beyond contemporary and reduced ideas of pleasure and happiness. It discovers something more powerful.

Such a life—staggering, according to Paul—delights in weaknesses, insults, opposition, and suffering. It embraces the rebellion of joy. The offense of those who partied with Jesus, causing the condemnation of the Pharisees, must not be read through contemporary eyes, tainted by recent ideas of Christian stodginess. It was not the drunkenness, or possibly carousing, that truly offended the Pharisees; it was the offense of their joy. The idea that tax collectors, lepers, and women forced into sex work could celebrate. *Their lives were accursed. They were destined to suffer and lament. How dare they be filled with joy?* The offensiveness of this joy lived in a life of difficulties and limitations still exists today. Yet to many, to those filled with fear, anxiety, and despair, the joy of those who have come to the end of themselves is a light on a hill—a life lived in the Spirit, a witness to the gospel.

Globalization and the Gospel

Freed from the slavery of self, and standing strong against the temptations of falling back into the elemental forces, and guarded against the temptation to run beyond Jesus into a self-driven freedom, we are now in a unique and powerful posture in our globalizing world. The clock cannot be turned back, our communities and nations cannot return to being sealed sanctuaries. They never really were. Instead, turning the force of Babel against itself, the life lived in the Spirit enables the church to spread the gospel on the back of globalization. The Roman Empire, a social and political empire of idolatry, centered around the worship of gods, and the power and drive of humans, was turned against itself. Its common languages of Greek and Latin used by the creative minority of the church to communicate the gospel across the world. Its roads, highways, and infrastructure facilitating apostolic steps. Its laws of citizenship, its law and order, used to protect apostles even as it martyred others.

Across the West, multiculturalism has brought the world to us; the nations to be discipled are now brushing up against us at the supermarket aisle. The church is becoming an example of the future diversity of heaven. Fighting the flesh, wary of the elemental forces, technology can again become a tool, placed in its proper place. Air travel and the Internet become new Roman roads for gospel passage. God working as He always has in the muck and mud of history, moving the world toward His purposes.

* * * * *

E. Stanley Jones is right when he says, "When we 'receive' the kingdom, then we work with the nature of things, we work with the grain of the universe, we co-operate with reality, hence life becomes effective and rhythmical."[4] The abundant life Jesus spoke of that comes with entry into the kingdom life of God, life becoming effective and rhythmical, is not simply a life of pleasant feelings. Instead of preaching, teaching, and modeling a caricatured Christianity that offers positive feelings and the fruits of the achievement society, life in the Spirit and the road to true biblical joy leads through a revolt against feelings being the highest human good. Sketching out the vision of the church, Paul speaks of a dynamic body of people, being brought together in radical new ways, exercising gifts given by the Spirit, growing in unity—a new humanity living by the Spirit.

A recently declassified intelligence document, which had been written during the Cold War, explains to field agents the kind of person who can be "turned" to commit treason and spy against their own country. [5] Agents were instructed to keep an eye out for those with emotional fragility, those who were immature and insecure, seeking to make an impact in order to gain a sense of worth, disconnected from a strong community, accountability, and deep relationships. In the mid 1960s such personalities were difficult to find. However, worryingly, today these traits are ubiquitous in the contemporary self and, as I described in the previous chapter, in the contemporary congregation.

A growing cohort of Christians, shaped by achievement society but attempting to live by faith, struggle to enjoy the complete suite of pleasures, freedoms, and possibilities promised by contemporary culture. Enslaved to emotions and the tyranny of feelings, they discover the bankruptcy of such an approach as they are tossed and swayed by the deceptive philosophies of our day—political, cultural, and religious programs, which at their roots fall back into the elemental forces, or post-Christian humanistic flights into destructive freedoms.

Paul speaks to this temptation when he tells the early church to adjust their life according to the reality of the gospel, "to put off your old self, which is being corrupted by it deceitful desires, to be made new in the attitude of your minds; and to put on the new self, created to be like God in true righteousness and holiness" (Eph. 4:22–24 NIV). Resilience comes from putting to death in you that which is not under the lordship of Christ. Meaning is found in the battle, the war between flesh and spirit. The great hope of the church in our world, straining in the tensions between place and non-place, freedom and falling back into the elemental forces, is a people walking in the life of God, being filled with His Spirit, crucifying the flesh daily, living as citizens of heaven and ambassadors of the kingdom, reflecting Christlikeness. This is the purpose of your life.

STRANGE DAYS

The early Christians were faced with the totality of Roman control of the public imagination. Surrounded by the Roman optics of majesty and grandeur. The magnificent temples, infrastructure, entertainments, lavish palaces, cities, and military forces, the early Christians could easily have been overwhelmed. For if ours is a digital age, theirs was a concrete age. The Romans were defined by their contribution to the craft of building. Rome initially overran people with legions and military power, but concrete sealed the deal. Swords conquered the body, but the cult of concrete overcame their soul. The Roman statesman and chronicler of imperial expansion Cassius Dio cannily understood this: "With cities being founded, and the barbarians adapting to a whole new way of living, they were on their way to becoming Roman."[1] A Roman was not so much an ethnicity, but an idea ingested, a habitual covenant with its concrete power.

Against this concrete, this touchable sacrament of human power, the Christians seemed (through human eyes at least) to have a limited arsenal. However, they were a people called.

They dealt not in the power of concrete, hard power, or civil religion. Instead, theirs was a relational craft. If there was a symbol among them to be found, it was the table. The pared down meal of bread and wine. The reconstituted humanity that gathered around the communion table was already present in the life of Jesus. Into a community, divided by the sacred borders that governed eating together, the feeding of the multitudes by Jesus anticipating the form the church would take, observes Bruce Bradshaw:

> Jesus reconciled the disparate people of a community to one another, empowering them to affirm one another's humanity, transforming the elements of the kosmos that governed their lives, including the religious, ethnic, political, social, and economic structures that separated. They shifted their image of themselves from "I am because they aren't" to "I am because we are," realizing that Christ transforms people into new creations. The church is composed of these new creations.[2]

The feast was not found in the food, it was found in the Lord, and the ability that He gave to see each other no longer as Roman or barbarian, male or female, Jew or Gentile, but as humans, each uniquely made and created.

The Empire, indeed as all empires are, was undone not by a frontal military assault, nor by a violent subversive insurgency, but rather by the breaking of the humblest of foods: bread. By the remembering of Christ and His work on the cross, through which He had overcome the world. Their revolution was staged not in the theaters, stadiums, or palaces; instead it was in the crowded streets, the huddled apartment complexes. Its power on display in the lives of saints. Ordinary saints, normal people, living out an extraordinary vision, a radical reordered society of humans around the lordship of Christ. A revolution not against flesh and blood, but powers and principalities. A vision of equality, surrounded by a new kind of boundary drawn not by human hands, but divine justice and holiness. Living in the tension of the end-times.

The church, this vision of humanity resurrected in Christ, this radical reordering of the elemental forces, this equality contained and buffeted in the church has lived through countless political systems, cultural configurations, and social movements. The cautionary tales of the book of Acts, the warnings against false teachers found in the Pastoral Epistles, the corrections and rebukes of Paul's writings, offer a realistic view of the church. A concert of people fighting the flesh, living through the Spirit. At times, just as Paul warned, falling back into the slavery of the elemental forces, at other times losing itself in the freedom, forgetting its source. As Christ promised Peter, that the gates of hell shall not prevail against the church, and in every age, the principalities and powers, humiliated and exposed could not contain its advance. And so it will continue to move forward in our age of upheaval; the gospel will continue to change hearts, the living laboratory of Spirit-filled life that is the church will grow and advance the kingdom in our time. So in our strange days when the anxiety starts to tighten my chest, I think of my Chinese brother in Christ, Ni Tuosheng, better known as Watchman Nee, who spent much of his life suffering for his faith in prison, separated from his wife and family, denounced by his friends. Across time, we are brothers. He is my mentor in the battle against the flesh, in this feverish feelings-driven moment, he reminds me that "The soul which comes under the Holy Spirit's authority is a restful one."[3]

In our strange days, as I watch the tensions of globalization, the never-ending stream of migrants and refugees, I think about the text from my friend in Europe, telling of shrinking Scandinavian and German churches now bursting at the seams with Syrian refugees coming to faith. I think of my small part of Melbourne, the hundreds of Iranians meeting Jesus. The Sudanese, Burmese, Chinese, Indian congregations springing up in the secular soil. I think of the army of ordinary believers I know quietly and lovingly welcoming, teaching English to, and befriending refugees with the love of Christ.

In our strange days of tensions, war, injustice, and poverty, I think of my countless brothers and sisters in Christ across the world, engaged in feeding the hungry, advocating for the voiceless, peacemaking in the conflict zones, ministering to the poor, each partnering with God, as the kingdom breaks out in this world. All off the radar of the 24-hour cable news cycle, yet resounding with trumpets of praise in heaven.

In our strange days, as secularism seems triumphant, in which an intolerant cultural tide in the West appears to be turning against Christianity, I think of the words of my British brother Joel Edwards, whose work is to defend the persecuted church. Joel preached in my church this last Sunday, that what we face in the West is not persecution but uncomfortability. As someone who walks the corridors of Western power, Joel shared that he is constantly confronted by the tensions that his evangelical, orthodox belief in Jesus' exclusivity creates as he goes about his work outside of the church. As he reminded my church, this tension should be embraced as a creative one, necessary and filled with possibility.

In our strange days, in which faith seems increasingly strange, in which the church in the West appears to be in retreat, I think of the atheists, agnostics, seekers, Muslims, Buddhists, dechurched, and New Agers who turn up to my church, brought by friends, or even just turning up alone, each drawn by something different they see in the love of the imperfect believers in our community. I think of those finding faith in our Alpha groups. I think of my sister in Christ, who just crossed the borderline of baptism as I wrote this chapter, initially repelled by what she thought was Christianity, yet who has now found Christ. I think of the same stories told in the flourishing churches of my friends, in the most secular cities in the West.

In our strange days, as I ask myself if our world has gone mad, as I worry at the trajectory of our world, of its politics, its conflicts, its injustices and lies, I remember that God has got this. And so I think of my brother in Christ, the apostle John, exiled on Patmos, whose words end the Bible as they will end my book:

> He who is the faithful witness to all these things says,
> "Yes I am coming soon!"
> Amen! Come Lord Jesus!
> May the grace of the Lord Jesus be with God's holy
> people.
> (Rev. 22:20–21 NLT)

NOTES

INTRODUCTION: RELAXING IN THE SKIES ABOVE THE ISLAMIC STATE

1. Richard N. Haass, "How to Respond to a Disordered World," *Foreign Affairs* (November/December 2014), https://www.foreignaffairs.com/articles/united-states/2014-10-20/unraveling.
2. Alain de Botton, *The News: A User's Manual* (New York: Pantheon, 2014), 16.
3. Ibid.
4. Douglas Rushkoff, *Present Shock: When Everything Happens Now* (New York: Current, 2013), 49.
5. Tania Branigan, "Mongolian Neo-Nazis: Anti-Chinese Sentiment Fuels Rise of Ultra-Nationalism," *The Guardian*, August 3, 2010, https://www.theguardian.com/world/2010/aug/02/mongolia-far-right.
6. Jason Burke, "'Racist' Gandhi Statue Banished from Ghana University Campus," *The Guardian*, October 7, 2016, https://www.theguardian.com/world/2016/oct/06/ghana-academics-petition-removal-mahatma-gandhi-statue-african-heroes.

CHAPTER 1: FROM EDEN TO THE EAST

1. Peter J. Leithart, *Delivered from the Elements of the World: Atonement, Justification, Mission* (Downers Grove, IL: InterVarsity Press, 2016), 41.
2. Jacques Ellul, *The Meaning of the City* (Grand Rapids: Eerdmans, 1970), 3.
3. Ibid., 5.
4. Leon R. Kass, *The Beginning of Wisdom: Reading Genesis* (Chicago: University of Chicago Press, 2003), 145.

CHAPTER 2: THE NATIONS RAGE

1. John Goldingay, *Psalms Volume 1: Psalms 1-41*, Baker Commentary on the Old Testament Wisdom and Psalms (Grand Rapids: Baker, 2006), 98.

2. Saint Augustine, *City of God* (London: Penguin, 1984), 549–50.

3. See Aristotle, *The Nicomachean Ethics*, Book 1.iii.

4. Tacitus illuminates for us that what are considered "modern" views of sex are millennia old. See Tacitus, *Germania*

5. Herman Ridderbos, Paul: An Outline of His Theology (Grand Rapids: Eerdmans, 1975), 103.

CHAPTER 3: THE RELIGIOUS ARCHITECTURE OF EVERY SOCIETY

1. Peter J. Leithart, *Delivered from the Elements of the World: Atonement, Justification, Mission* (Downers Grove, IL: InterVarsity Press, 2016), 11.

2. Ibid., 12.

3. Ibid.

4. Mary Douglas, *Purity and Danger: An Analysis of the Concepts of Purity and Taboo* (New York: Routledge, 1966), 122.

5. Benjamin Barber, *Jihad vs. McWorld: Terrorism's Challenge to Democracy* (New York: Ballantine Books, 1996), 4.

6. Thomas L. Friedman, *The Lexus and the Olive Tree* (New York: Anchor, 2000), 9.

7. See Ulrich Beck, Anthony Giddens, Scott Lash, *Reflexive Modernization: Politics, Tradition and Aesthetics in the Modern Social Order* (Stanford, CA: Stanford University Press, 1994), 96.

8. Friedman, 9.

9. See John R. Schindler, "The White House Just Charted a Dangerous Course With NSC Machinations," *The Observer*, January 30, 2017, http://observer.com/2017/01/donald-trump-bannon-flynn-national-security-coup/.

CHAPTER 4: CIVILIZATIONS STRIVING

1. Quoted in *Archie Brown, The Rise and Fall of Communism* (London: Vintage, 2009), 524.

2. Quoted in Tim Weiner, *Legacy of Ashes: The History of the CIA* (New York, Doubleday, 2007), 429.

3. Jesus Jones, "Right Here, Right Now," written by Michael Edwards, Sony/ATV Music Publishing LLC, Universal Music Publishing Group.

4. Christopher Dawson, *Progress and Religion* (New York: Image Books, 1960), 14.

5. Quoted in Chris Bowlby, "Vladimir Putin's Formative German Years," BBC News, March 27, 2015, http://www.bbc.com/news/magazine-32066222.

6. Ben Judah, *Fragile Empire: How Russia Fell In and Out of Love with Vladimir Putin* (London: Yale University Press, 2013), 15.

7. Francis Fukuyama, *The End of History and the Last Man* (New York: The Free Press, 1992), xvi.

8. Quoted in Jean M. Twenge, *Generation Me: Why Today's Young Americans Are More Confident, Assertive, Entitled—and More Miserable Than Ever Before* (New York: Free Press, 2006), 83.

9. See *Generation Me*.

10. Robert Kagan, *The Return of History and the End of Dreams* (New York: Alfred A. Knopf, 2008), 3.

11. See Robert D. Kaplan, *The Revenge of Geography: What the Map Tells Us About Coming Conflicts and the Battle Against Fate* (New York: Random House, 2012), chapter 1.

CHAPTER 5: NON-PLACES, PRAYER CLOSETS OF INDIVIDUALISM

1. Tom McCarthy, *Satin Island* (New York: Vintage, 2015), 6.

2. Marc Auge, *Non-Places: Introduction to an Anthropology of Supermodernity* (London: Verso, 1995), 38.

3. Andrew Sullivan, "I Used to Be a Human Being," *New York*, September 18, 2016, http://nymag.com/selectall/2016/09/andrew-sullivan-technology-almost-killed-me.html.

4. Quoted in Eric Barker, "This Is How To Resist Distraction: 4 Secrets To Remarkable Focus," *Barking Up the Wrong Tree* (blog), October 2, 2016, http://www.bakadesuyo.com/2016/10/how-to-resist-distraction/.

5. James K. A. Smith, *Desiring the Kingdom: Worship, Worldview, and Cultural Formation* (Grand Rapids: Baker, 2009), 25.

6. Ibid.

7. Kate Lunau, "Campus Crisis: The Broken Generation. Why So Many of Our Best and Brightest Students Report Feeling Hopeless, Depressed, Even Suicidal," *Maclean's* magazine, September 5, 2012, http://www.macleans.ca/news/canada/the-broken-generation/.

8. Byung-Chul Han, *The Burnout Society* (Stanford, CA: Stanford University Press, 2015), 36.

9. Ibid., 42.

10. Ibid., 50–51.

CHAPTER 6: TERRORISM

1. Lawrence Wright, *The Looming Tower: Al-Qaeda's Road To 9/11* (London: Penguin, 2006), 91–92.

2. Robert Lacey, *Inside the Kingdom: Kings, Clerics, Modernists, Terrorists and the Struggle for Saudi Arabia* (London: Hutchinson, 2009), 14.

3. Quoted in Christian Caryl, *Strange Rebels: 1979 and the Birth of the 21st Century* (New York: Basic, 2014), 46.

4. Quoted in Wright, *The Looming Tower*, 47.

5. See John Merriman, *The Dynamite Club: How a Bombing in Fin-De-Siecle Paris Ignited the Age of Modern Terror* (London: JR Books, 2009).

6. Jessica Stern and J.M. Berger, *ISIS: The State of Terror* (London: William Collins, 2015), 69.

7. Ibid., 279.

8. Ibid., 76.

CHAPTER 7: POLARIZED POLITICS

1. Roger Scruton, *Fools, Frauds and Firebrands: Thinkers of the New Left* (London: Bloomsbury, 2015), 99.

2. Alasdair Macintyre, *Herbert Marcuse: An Exposition and a Polemic* (New York: Viking, 1970), 100.

3. Ibid.

4. Greg Lukianoff and Jonathan Haidt, "The Coddling of the American Mind," *The Atlantic*, September 2015, http://www.theatlantic.com/magazine/archive/2015/09/the-coddling-of-the-american-mind/399356.

5. Emily Gosden, "Student Accused of Violating University 'Safe Space' by Raising Her Hand," *The Telegraph*, April 3, 2016, http://www.telegraph.co.uk/news/2016/04/03/student-accused-of-violating-university-safe-space-by-raising-he/.

6. Other members of the radical Japanese New Left would relocate to Lebanon and form the feared Japanese Red Army, one of the 1970s' most feared terrorist groups in the world. The group would offer themselves as guns for hire, committing terrorist attacks across the world, most famously the Lod Airport massacre.

7. Francis Fukuyama, *The End of History and the Last Man* (New York: Free Press, 1992), 314.

8. For more on this, see Martin Jay, *The Dialectical Imagination: A History of the Frankfurt School and the Institute of Social Research, 1923-1950* (Berkeley and Los Angeles: University of California Press, 1973), chapter 2.

9. See James Parker, "Donald Trump, Sex Pistol: The punk-rock appeal of the GOP nominee," *The Atlantic*, October 2016, http://www.theatlantic.com/magazine/archive/2016/10/donald-trump-sex-pistol/497528/.

10. Matt Lees, "See What Gamergate Should Have Taught Us About the 'Alt-Right,'" *The Guardian*, December 1, 2016, https://www.theguardian.com/technology/2016/dec/01/gamergate-alt-right-hate-trump.

11. See Amanda Marcotte, "The Alt-Right Attacks Sci-Fi: How the Hugo Awards Got Hijacked by Trumpian-Style Culture Warriors," *Salon*, August 24, 2016, http://www.salon.com/2016/08/23/the-alt-right-attacks-sci-fi-how-the-hugo-awards-got-hijacked-by-trumpian-style-culture-warriors/.

12. See Aja Romano, "How the Alt-Right Uses Internet Trolling To Confuse You Into Dismissing Its Ideology, *Vox*, January 11, 2017, http://www.vox.com/2016/11/23/13659634/alt-right-trolling.

13. Andrew Keen, *The Cult of the Amateur: How Blogs, Myspace, YouTube, and the Rest of Today's User-Generated Media are Destroying Our Economy, Our Culture, and Our Values* (New York: Doubleday, 2006), 17.

14. On July 21, 2016, Ross Douthat (@DouthatNY) tweeted, "The Trumpian right and the SJW left are our first real intimations of what a genuinely post-Christian politics might look like."

CHAPTER 8: CULTURAL DIFFUSION

1. Plato, *Republic*, 555b–576d.

2. See Abd Ar Rahman bin Muhammed ibn Khaldun, *The Muqaddimah*, chapter 2, section 14.

3. Alexis de Tocqueville, *Democracy in America*, Part Two, Book IV.

4. Moises Naim, *The End of Power: From Boardrooms to Battlefields and Churches to States. Why Being in Charge Isn't What it Used to Be* (New York: Basic, 2013), 34.

5. William H. David, *Overconnected: Where to Draw the Line at Being Online* (London: Hachette, 2011), Kindle loc. 145.

6. Yuval Levin, *The Fractured Republic: Renewing America's Social Contract in the Age of Individualism* (New York: Basic Books, 2016), 169–172.

CHAPTER 9: CHURCH IN BATTLE

1. Walter Lippmann, *The Phantom Public* (New Brunswick, NJ: Transaction, 1993), 56.

2. See Peter J. Leithart, *Delivered from the Elements of the World: Atonement, Justification, Mission* (Downers Grove, IL: InterVarsity Press, 2016), 37.

3. Ibid.

4. Michael W. Goheen, *Introducing Christian Mission Today: Scripture, History and Issues* (Downers Grove, IL: InterVarsity Press, 2014), 419.

5. Michael Knowles, "An Actual Conservative's Guide to the Alt-Right: 8 Things You Need to Know," *The Daily Wire*, September 26, 2016, http://www.dailywire.com/news/9441/actual-conservatives-guide-alt-right-8-things-you-michael-knowles

6. For more on this effect of the blitz, see Malcolm Gladwell, *David and Goliath: Underdogs, Misfits, and the Art of Battling Giants* (New York: Little, Brown, and Company, 2013).

7. See Ben Schott, "The Immigrant Paradox," *New York Times*, September 29, 2010, https://schott.blogs.nytimes.com/2010/09/29/the-immigrant-paradox/?_r=0.

8. Jacques Ellul, *Violence: Reflections from a Christian Perspective* (New York: Seabury, 1969), 166–170.

9. Leithart, *Delivered from the Elements of the World*, 289.

CHAPTER 10: LIFE IN THE SPIRIT

1. Charles Williams, *Descent of the Dove: A Short History of the Holy Spirit in the Church* (Grand Rapids: Eerdmans, 1974), 3.

2. Ibid.

3. Ibid.

4. Ibid.

5. Wayne A. Meeks, *The First Urban Christians: The Social World of the Apostle Paul* (New Haven, CT: Yale University Press, 1983), 102.

6. James S. Jeffers, *The Greco-Roman World of the New Testament: Exploring the Background of Early Christianity* (Downers Grove, IL: InterVarsity Press, 1999), 79–80.

7. Arthur F. Glasser, Charles E. Van Engen, Dean S. Gilliland, and Shawn B. Redford, *Announcing the Kingdom: The Story of God's Mission in the Bible* (Grand Rapids: Baker, 2003), 339.

8. Marva J. Dawn, *Powers, Weakness, and the Tabernacling of God* (Grand Rapids: Eerdmans, 2001), 126.

CHAPTER 11: TRANSGRESSING BOUNDARIES

1. Lesslie Newbigin, *A Word in Season: Perspectives on Christian World Missions* (Grand Rapids: Eerdmans, 1994), 153.

2. Leithart, *Delivered from the Elements of the World*, 281.

3. F. F. Bruce, *Paul: Apostle of the Heart Set Free* (Grand Rapids: Eerdmans, 1977), 183.

4. See Geoffrey Hosking, *Russia and the Russians: From Earliest Times to 2001* (London: Penguin, 2001), 484–86.

5. Herman Bavinck, quoted in John Bolt, *Bavinck on the Christian Life: Following Jesus in Faithful Service* (Wheaton, IL: Crossway, 2015), 157–58.

6. Baron F. Von Hugel, *Letters to a Niece* (London: Fount, 1995), 13.

7. Newbigin, *A Word in Season*, 153.

8. Andrew Keen, *Digital Vertigo: How Today's Online Social Revolution is Dividing, Diminishing, and Disorientating Us* (New York: St. Martins, 2012), 108.

CHAPTER 12: WHAT KIND OF EXILE IS THIS?

1. Thomas A. Kempis, *The Imitation of Christ* (London: Penguin, 1952), 39.

2. Edwin Schur, *The Awareness Trap: Self-Absorption Instead of Social Change* (New York: McGraw-Hill, 1977), 58.

3. E. Stanley Jones, *Is the Kingdom of God Realism?* (New York: Abingdon-Cokesbury, 1940), 63.

4. R. Kent Hughes, *Luke: That You May Know the Truth* (Wheaton, IL: Crossway, 2015), 95–96.

CHAPTER 13: ON EARTH AS IT IS IN HEAVEN

1. De Civitate Dei, illustration showing Paradise in the French 15th Century Manuscript in the Bibliotheque Sainte-Genevieve, Paris.

2. Peter Brown, *The World of Late Antiquity* (New York: W.W. Norton & Company, Inc., 1989), 50.

3. Ibid., 51–52.

4. E. Stanley Jones, *Is the Kingdom of God Realism?* (New York: Abingdon-Cokesbury, 1940), 64.

5. See Gordon Corera, *The Art of Betrayal: Life and Death in the British Secret Service* (London: Orion, 2011), 181.

CONCLUSION: STRANGE DAYS

1. Cassius Dio, quoted in Tom Holland, *Dynasty: The Rise and Fall of the House of Caesar* (London: Abacus, 2015), 165.

2. Bruce Bradshaw, *Change Across Cultures: A Narrative Approach to Social Transformation* (Grand Rapids: Baker, 2002), 209–210.

3. Watchman Nee, *The Spiritual Man* (New York: Christian Fellowship Publishers, 1968), 205.

ACKNOWLEDGMENTS

I t has become popular to list in your acknowledgments albums and music that one has listened to while writing. Yes, I did listen to music while writing this book, but the true soundtrack that should be acknowledged is the sound of my family and my church. This is my sixth book, but I am still deeply grateful as always to my wonderful family for their support and to Red Church. Thanks also to my faithful readers Sarah and Glen, plus John Mark who also offered feedback, as well as the fantastic team at Moody: Randall, Matthew, and Connor. The spark for this book comes from the interplay of doing ministry and leading here in Melbourne, with all the blessings and challenges that brings. It grew into a concrete idea as I jetted off for my lightning visits to the Northern Hemisphere, as I do a couple times a year. As I travelled through airports and cities in Europe and America, two books deeply shaped how I thought about what I was seeing. Firstly, Tom McCarthy's novel *Satin Island*, which attempts to capture the phenomenon of being human at this time in global culture. In my other hand was Peter Leithart's *Delivered From the Elements of the World*, a rich and brilliant work. Two other books deserve a mention for inspiration: Shadia B. Drury's work on Alexandre Kojève, and Peter Pomerantsev's *Nothing is True and Everything is Possible*. Lastly, as always I am left at the end of the writing process with an ever deeper and more profound appreciation of God's glory, love, and grace. To Him be all the praise..

ALSO BY
MARK SAYERS

FROM **MOODYPUBLISHERS.COM**

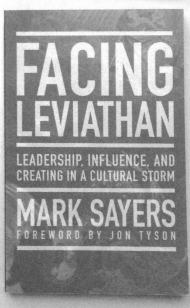

a book
by Mark Sayers

THE ROAD TRIP
THAT CHANGED THE WORLD

THE UNLIKELY THEORY THAT
WILL CHANGE HOW YOU VIEW
CULTURE, THE CHURCH, AND
MOST IMPORTANTLY, **YOURSELF**

978-0-8024-0931-7

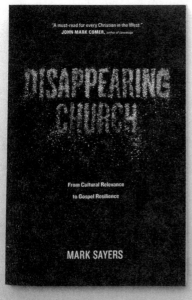

"A must-read for every Christian in the West".
JOHN MARK COMER, *author of Loveology*

DISAPPEARING
CHURCH

**From Cultural Relevance
to Gospel Resilience**

MARK SAYERS

978-0-8024-1335-2

FACING
LEVIATHAN

LEADERSHIP, INFLUENCE, AND
CREATING IN A CULTURAL STORM

MARK SAYERS

FOREWORD BY JON TYSON

978-0-8024-1096-2

ALSO AVAILABLE AS EBOOKS